Howard Barker

PLAYS SEVEN

Und

The Twelfth Battle of Isonzo

12 Encounters With a Prodigy

Christ's Dog

Learning Kneeling

OBERON BOOKS
LONDON

WWW.OBERONBOOKS.COM

First published in this collection 2012
by Oberon Books Ltd
521 Caledonian Road, London N7 9RH
Tel: +44 (0) 20 7607 3637 / Fax: +44 (0) 20 7607 3629
e-mail: info@oberonbooks.com
www.oberonbooks.com

A catalogue record for this book is available from the British Library.

PB ISBN: 978-1-84943-401-0
E ISBN: 978-1-84943-697-7

Cover image by Eduardo Houth

Printed, bound and converted
by CPI Group (UK) Ltd, Croydon, CR0 4YY.

Visit www.oberonbooks.com to read more about all our books
and to buy them. You will also find features, author interviews and
news of any author events, and you can sign up for e-newsletters
so that you're always first to hear about our new releases.

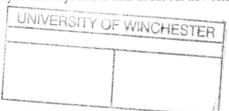

Contents

UND

(An interior. A tea-tray, laden. A woman waits for a man.)

UND: He's late
(Pause.)
He's late
(Pause.)
Scarcely
Scarcely late at all
But late
(Pause.)
Now is this fractional lateness merely the first
instalment of considerable lateness or is it
(Pause.)
Purely fractional?
(Pause.)
Fractional lateness which will lose any
significance the moment he
(Pause.)
Still fractional
(Pause.)
Not so fractional now
(Pause.)
The dilemma for a man of his extraordinary
stature is this surely surely this that lateness
whilst it may serve to demonstrate disdain for
all those petty and conventional narrow and
restrictive disciplines to which so many of us are
still subject might it not also indicate
*(The swift descent of a mirror. It hangs before her face,
reflecting it to the audience. She observes herself.)*
Oh
Oh
Oh
Am I not an ecstasy of
A delirium of
And a convulsion of perfection which

9

HAIR OUT OF PLACE

(She laughs.)

Not really

Not really

Go away

I did not ring

Out

Out

Servants oh

They have no humour but how could they have
what humour is compatible with service

THIS IS QUITE LATE NOW

(Pause.)

And I am not ashamed to say that I attach as
much importance to the expressions of sincerity
as I attach to the sincerity itself

IS THAT NOT PROFOUNDLY ARCHAIC

Who cares if it's archaic much of me is archaic

I am a fragment of a dying class whose archaism
is

AND POSSIBLY ALWAYS WAS

The source of its fascination

I'm talking about manners

(Pause.)

Of which he is in dire need it seems

(*Pause.*)

And he has telephones oh not one not half a
dozen but entire switchboards yes room on
room the wires the plugs the sockets

(Pause.)

But I dislike the telephone I always have and he

(Pause.)

How thoughtful and considerate he

(Pause.)

That coarse and brutal bell he possibly intuits I
would not welcome even an apology delivered
by such means the violation of placid and
fragrant domesticity no his failure to explain his
lateness is evidence of fine feeling fine at least
regarding telephones

REMOVE THE TEA TRAY

*(She turns inside the gown, presenting her head and
shoulders to the audience.)*

I am not not not furious

Why should I be

The world's peculiar not me

The world is this demeaning spectacle not me

DON'T REMOVE IT

(Pause.)

Removing it endows the whole occasion with
significance as if I could not bear the sight of
it before me no let it gather dust someone will
collect it at some point perhaps tomorrow or
the cat will knock it off oh dear I'll say sugar oh
dear milk on all the furniture how long has that
tray been there abandoned like a tennis court
in winter the occasion having been the pretext
having been erased from memory

(Pause.)

He gathers Jews

(Pause.)

The dress oh that the dress yes possibly of all the
gowns it is the most extravagant I don't conceal
it from myself I choose this to

(Pause.)

OVERWHELM

(Pause.)

If such a man can be

If such a man is ever

And I am perfectly aware men do not care for
the extremes of female fashion oh yes perfectly
aware it wounds them in some way except for
homosexuals
(Pause.)
They like it
They really do
Extravagance oh
Excess
Oh
Oh
How vulgar
How discerning
Both
Simultaneous
Oh
Homosexuals
They
(Pause.)
The air he walked through was not still but
shook with contrary winds small winds gusting
winds which plucked his tunic or pressed his
trousers flat against his hips and through these
winds perhaps the cause of them sailed bands
sailed hoops of tungsten razor sharp bowling
and bouncing sometimes colliding any one of
which could slice through flesh and bone divide
a man in half behead lop trim and singing
always singing this acquired a certain beauty so
he said
(She perambulates.)
And what was the horizon for want of a better
word the horizon rose and fell in constant
motion fountains geysers boiling plunging liquid
volatile all seen through tidal heat and rolling

clouds of toxins livid bile and copper green and
this acquired a certain beauty so he said
(She perambulates.)
Into this he walked walked walked he did not
run and where he encountered obstacles lifted
his leg placing the sole of his boot firmly in
the ground neither stooping nor attempting to
present the narrow profile of his body to the
front his shirt unbuttoned and wearing a soft cap
not a helmet in one hand a cane and in the other
nothing nothing nothing in the other hand
(She stops.)
Which
Surely
He
Clenched
As
A
Fist
(Pause.)
Or not not even this but let hang loosely fingers
idly vertical as if in summer streets he saw a cafe
with a green tin table and passing between trams
dreamed a coffee dreamed a cigarette certainly
he held his hand like this certainly I imagine
certainly and the dead
(Pause.)
TAKE THIS TRAY AWAY
(Pause.)
I shout these orders no one comes it is as if she
can detect so subtly is her character attuned to
mine it is only chagrin that is indicated pique
and all that's infantile in her beloved mistress
and much is much is infantile in me I confess I
would not wish it otherwise have you met the
adult have you spent time with the thoroughly
mature

Oh

Oh

Their oceanic wisdom suffocates your soul

(Pause.)

The dead acquired a certain beauty
notwithstanding their agonized expressions
twisted limbs eviscerations a certain beauty so
he said

(A faint ring.)

THAT'S HIM THERE'S THE BELL

Late

Late

And that sort of lateness which the very worst
of all which spoils the carefully constructed
compensations of an unexpected solitude

LET HIM STAND THERE LET HIM IF IT IS
HIM SUFFER

I am

Whilst thoroughly prepared

Now

Not

Prepared

At

All

How refined oh how refined he is if not in
manners in those oscillations of the social which
can wreck your nerves

PERFECT TIMING IF YOU WANT TO
TOPPLE SOMEONE'S GUARD

(She is still. The bell rings.)

THERE IT IS AGAIN

Don't go

Don't go

The slightest who but me would register the
slightest irritation in the pulling of the rope

He is fatigued

He

If it is him

Possibly perspires at this prospect of the door
not ever being opened now

His lateness being fractionally

For all its calibration

Fractionally excessive and far from playing
with my nerves has caused profound and
inextinguishable offence

Manipulation

Oh I know manipulation

It's an art

(The bell.)

NOW THAT IS TEMPER

(Pause.)

That

(Pause.)

That is trade

Coal

Coke

Butchery

WHY DON'T YOU GO

I didn't hear a van

I didn't hear a lorry

But by the same token nor did I hear a car

IT IS NOT HIM IT IS A LOUT

Unless

Unless

He is so fictional so utterly the product of his
own byzantine will that he has chosen to cloak
his sensibility in this

(The bell.)

THAT IS NO WAY TO TREAT A BELL

Why don't you go

Why don't you stop him

Say the bell will
Say the bell is only
No
Say we'll pay
(Pause.)
The Jews exhaust him probably
(Pause.)
At the end of a day he flings himself down on a
bed a simple bed he prefers beds to be simple
not more than a cot or is it canvas with a blanket
flat no pillow and sleeps such sleeps but not of
great duration brief and deep such as he slept
under bombardment in a hole in water even
cold rain hunger notwithstanding and wakes
restored to
(Pause.)
VIGOUR
I'LL WRITE TO HIM
I WILL
I CAN
The quality of aristocracy is this that whereas
all other classes are inhabited by stifling
conventions they choose to call morality we
make law of our appetites murder for example
take the Hohenzollerns did you ever see a worse
the Esterhazys their portraits say it all those
English what are they the Tudors and the Sforzas
why shouldn't I send him a note sarcastic
obviously in my sloping hand and ink splashed
as if I were so full of so sodden in disdain I
smudged and spotted it yes I know how to
wound
(Pause.)
The patience of the Jews I marvel
(The bell.)
YOU SEE HE HAS NOT GONE AWAY

I dislike this

This has acquired the character of

There is no other word for it

A CONTEST

I don't mind

Oh I can

Yes

It doesn't disconcert my

Not at all

I'm not averse to these what are they certainly
not games but not seductions either

MANIFESTATIONS OF FRUSTRATED
WILL

DISCONNECT THE BELL

(Pause.)

It's a wire the wire runs through a dozen loops
she only has to

(The bell.)

DISCONNECT I SAID

Or where the levers join two sections simply
lift a child could do it lift the cable off the
manufacturer anticipated occasions such as this
in rural districts lunatics might plague your life
of mischievous relatives they can cause you
sleepless nights the bell designer obviously
included in his patent the wherewithal to

OR DID HE THINK HIS BELL SO
SONOROUS SO PERFECT TO THE EAR
WE COULD NOT BUT DELIGHT NO
MATTER HOW EXCESSIVELY IT RANG

I'm under siege

(Pause.)

A character so resolute as his will hardly flinch
at the discovery a maid has resorted to the
expedient of unhooking the bell

RATHER THIS WILL STIMULATE HIS
APPETITE
I'll pour the tea
Not his
My own
It's cold
So what
Cold tea
Cold tea alone
I prefer it
It agrees with me
I pour
I stir
The perfect afternoon
So rarely do I need another's company
The effort to communicate oh
And posing questions purely to stimulate some
No
No
It's vastly preferable to be
*(A shattering of glass…UND is still… Only her eyes
register her alarm… She sips again.)*
Troy was terrible I imagine
Ten years that went on whole families were
exterminated Homer makes it somehow
glamorous but once the gates were down
And Magdeburg
Put to the sword
Vienna
TWICE
Paris they consumed the elephants
And Plevna everybody froze
(A second shattering of glass. She sips…)
The siege is desire
Desire

Expressed

As

Rage

(Pause.)

The most perfect form of sensuality is surely
this that culture whilst it cloaks instinct in a rigid
code decorum manners etiquette etcetera can
never wholly sublimate a certain passion for
barbarity

(A third shattering.)

CONNECT THE WIRES AGAIN

The bell is vastly preferable

Tell him

Write it on a note

Say

I'VE DROPPED THE CUP

MILK

TEA

OH

DAMN

OH

DAMN

DAMN

Ignore me

Just restore the bell

THE BELL FIRST THEN MY CLOTHES

Servants

Servants

Naturally they are susceptible to the slightest
inflections of my voice the merest indication
of hysteria and naturally they rush they fall
over one another it can't be helped they are
perfectly incapable of recognizing the priorities
demanded by the crisis if it is a crisis how could
they would they not in making such initiatives
fatally compromise their servitude it would be

tantamount to mutiny if on their own account
they chose the sequence in which

(The bell rings.)

WELL DONE

They chose to carry out their orders

(Pause.)

I say well done

(Pause.)

Well done I say but

(Pause.)

Was the bell

(Pause.)

I have to ask

(Pause.)

Ever disconnected in the first place?

(Pause.)

And my knees are soaked

(Pause.)

Soaked

(Pause.)

Knees

(Pause.)

Is it not just as likely that becoming bored
by breaking windows he chose for reasons of
variety to pluck the bell rope as he was passing
passing from one side of the house looking for
bricks from one side to the other end

(Shattering glass.)

Yes

Yes

(And the bell.)

Certainly that is the case

My fine intelligence will be the death of me

MY DRESS

A CLOTH

A SPONGE

I'm not an aristocrat I am a Jew

He is at least consistent and the evidence of
his consistency is this that the shattering of
windows whilst associated with delinquency is
not circumscribed by it and like every action is
susceptible to

(A shattering of glass.)

Interpretation

THAT IS NOT A HOOLIGAN

Never

Never

A hooligan that

But rather the deliberation of a disciplined and
beautiful mind which was able to contemplate its
own extinction walking walking walking into the
mouth of death as if in summer streets he saw a
cafe with a green tin table and passing between
trams dreamed a coffee dreamed a cigarette just
such an attitude of mind characterizes the way in
which these bricks are thrown oh yes

(Pause.)

The Jew possesses all the qualities of aristocracy

(Pause.)

Abundantly

(Pause.)

Possibly to excess but whether she can ever

THE DRAUGHT

BOARD UP THE WINDOWS

OR IF NOT BOARD NEWSPAPER

LET HIM SEE

LET HIM SEE THE CASUAL AND
UNHURRIED MANNER IN WHICH YOU
TAPE THE NEWSPAPER OVER THE
GLASS

MAKE A POINT OF IT

Obviously he cannot fail to recognize we also
are
Oh yes
WE DO NOT LACK DECORUM
Quick it's cold in here
Never mind my knees
My knees can wait
Knees later
I've got a handkerchief
Always
In my sleeve
(Pause.)
That's smoke
(Pause.)
Smoke
(Pause.)
IS THAT SMOKE?
(Pause. Her eyes move anxiously. She inhales…)
How he longs for me to panic it's a passion in
him
And I could
I could panic
I could satisfy him very easily
IS THE TELEPHONE IN ORDER BY THE
WAY
Could but will not
STOP WHATEVER YOU ARE DOING
LEAVE THE NEWSPAPERS
SO MANY ORDERS
AND OFTEN CONTRADICTORY I KNOW
CEASE PAPERING THE WINDOWS AND
FETCH THE PHONE
(She inhales.)
Horrid smell
Fumes

Fumes of what I do not know

Cloth

Horsehair

Kipper boxes

I hate to call the fire brigade it seems so

Think of them running

Scrambling into uniform

The urgency

The honourable and decent urgency of firemen

I cannot rid myself of the

AND THIS IS SURELY A MARK OF MY
DISCERNMENT

The feeling we should be able to solve problems
on our own

Yes

That's nobility

DON'T RING DON'T

(She laughs.)

The lower orders panic the lower orders have
no conscience police firemen soldiers oh they
don't hesitate

(She coughs.)

My eyes are watering

I'm crying

Absurd

(She holds a handkerchief to her eyes.)

Perfectly absurd

AND HOT

It's rather hot in here or is it me I'm hot the heat
is me and no wonder yes I am perspiring he is
certainly gaining an ascendency

I'LL UNDRESS A LITTLE

UNDRESS ME

LEAVE THE WINDOWS AND

I will sit here in my petticoat why not

Peculiar

Peculiar

His choice not mine perhaps he likes

QUICK

Half-naked

Two can play at that game the trick is this the trick is NOT TO BE as I appear to be NOT TO BE rendered foolish by the antics of another that is a mark of aristocracy

(Pause.)

The smoke however is

(Pause.)

The smoke is

(Pause.)

One gets used to smoke my uncle burned the stubble in October what a hideous oh I hated it the odour of burned straw it clung to everything you took a dress out of the wardrobe oh and if the wind was blowing in your direction oh

(Pause.)

And this is worse than straw straw at least seems natural

I'LL SEE TO MYSELF DON'T YOU

She's clumsy

She catches you in zips

Treads on hems and so on

(The bell.)

Better altogether if I undress myself

I DO ADMIRE THOSE WHO

MORE THAN TALENT MORE THAN BEAUTY

THOSE WHO

Simply

Walk

Walk

Walk

Into

(Pause.)

The terrible

(Pause.)

It is possible to value life more highly than life itself deserves

(Pause.)

He knew that

It was a mark of his absolute discernment that whilst it was always possible even at the moment of exposing himself to death even then at the precise second the bombardment ceased even then to discover some pretext for not

Not

Not

Always being available

Not

Always whispering in your ear

Nevertheless he walked

He did not run and where his leg encountered obstacles lifted his leg placing the sole of his boot firmly in the ground neither stooping nor attempting to present the narrow profile of his body to the front

A MILLION REASONS FOR NOT WALKING CAME INTO HIS MIND

He was however

Not intimidated by the fact of his or anyone's existence

(Pause.)

And nor am I

(Pause.)

We were destined for each other

Yes

WE SHARE SO MANY OH SO MANY IF NOT ALL

(A shattering blow of a hammer on a door. She is still.
Alarm is visible on her face.)

He is

Oh so

Implacable

(She laughs. She stops. The hammering again.)

That door is not

I've opened it a thousand times

Not made to be

(The bell.)

The bell…!

The bell is

Despite a certain

In the way he handles it a certain brusqueness

The bell is

MUSIC

(She laughs.)

Music of a sort

I don't object to it

Let him

IT'S MADE FOR RINGING AFTER ALL

(It rings again.)

Yes

Dear man…!

(And again.)

He demonstrates an extraordinary capacity for
violence and

(Again.)

Tenderness

(Again.)

I call that tenderness

It could be

(Again.)

More tender still but given the

(Again.)

Oh, that is tender
Yes
(Again.)
Oh, that is scarcely audible…as if…as if it
were…an adieu
DON'T LET HIM GO
(Pause.)
How quiet it is and odourless how stagnant
still and under glass thick weed has grown
thick as the wrist and with cruel calyxes no
one could penetrate and once the ivy has
reached to the chimney top we shall effectively
have disappeared the last few children who
remembered vaguely that a house was here
took trains some died it is a matter of the purest
speculation whether even one survived the girls
were sent to factories and the factories were you
know factories certainly the boys who joined the
army were the luckier despite the losses it's true
to say the boys
(Pause.)
One might be seated in the bottom of a pool
(Pause.)
A lifeless pool
(Pause.)
A pool in which
(Pause.)
Poisonous perhaps or so inordinately deep no
organism vegetation or
(Pause.)
Only a few relics of less happy times OH YES
THERE WERE LESS HAPPY TIMES OH
YES LESS LESS CONSIDERABLY LESS
(Pause.)
Silver plates a brooch a stallion's skull things
flung by those who fled or parts of those who

were the cause of flight the persecuted and the
persecutor same wet grave same
TAKE A LETTER SAYING I APOLOGIZE
He is extremely busy you will need to
perservere
Locate his office first
Don't wander aimlessly
Don't talk to those who do not know
It's obvious who knows it always is
The knowing have a quality
Authority is visible
The head the arms the hands
Even the hair
I do believe even the hair
QUITE POSSIBLY IT WILL REQUIRE
WHOLE DAYS AND NIGHTS QUITE
POSSIBLY
Snatch sleeps in chairs and always be first in the
queue
THE PROPER QUEUE HOWEVER NOT
THE
You know there are queues and queues
The queue which is pervaded by a certain air
Study the heads
The heads must be tilted up not down
OH, YOU KNOW QUEUES...!
(She laughs. Pause.)
My apology is not absolute there have
been faults on either side his arrogance is
insupportable but then possibly so is my pride
I'll make an inventory of our mutual errors his
work preoccupies him but a perfectly composed
an elegantly written letter oh they aren't
common it's not every day a finely conceived
communication of this sort drops in your tray
DO NOT DROP IT IN HIS TRAY

It must be placed directly in his hand
(A tray bearing paper, pen and ink enters, idly moving as a pendulum. She watches it. It ceases.)
Paper is it not
White paper is it not a sign of such
And ink
They talk of machinery but ink
The telephone but ink
(Pause.)
Not a long letter
(She takes the pen from the tray.)
On the contrary a single word
Yes
Oh the terrible power of a single word
Black
Scrawl
On
White
(Pause.)
Which word however
Which
Or does the word not matter then word
perhaps is immaterial what matters is the word's
appearance on the page
Its angled its dishevelled form
A WORD CAN BE DISHEVELLED
Oh yes not only hair a word take DOG
(She scrawls.)
It won't be dog dog would imply resentment
dog would cause him to conclude he had
offended me an aristocrat is never offended no
not dog I chose dog out the blue I chose dog at
random mat would do the same say mat
(She scrawls on a fresh sheet.)
There

A blot or two implying impatience or contempt

Not mat however

No

Not mat

SHE THINKS SHE IS A MAT

I do not

I am no one's mat

GRASS SAY

(She scrawls.)

Grass at a steeply angled gradient grass leaning violently and so indented so very passionate he could not fail to

(She takes another sheet.)

Or the opposite

GRASS FALLING BACKWARDS

Grass toppling off the page

Grass

Yes

It seems random but with so much that is random it contains

(Pause.)

Precisely

That

(Pause.)

Which

(She erupts into profound weeping. Her howl echoes through the house. It stops as if it anticipated the sound that follows. A tray appears and swings tantalizingly. On it lies a single letter…she is quite still…the pendulum of the tray at last comes to rest…)

Oh

His

Supreme

Oh

HANDKERCHIEF

This one is

Just look

Soddened

HANDKERCHIEF

The way one plucks a letter off a tray

should certainly reflect the true nobility of the

transaction

*(She lifts the letter off the tray. She produces
a paperknife from her clothing. She waits, the
instrument poised…)*

It is

I daresay

A communication of one word

Oh yes

He is not superfluous

A man who walked walked walked through

death and where his leg encountered obstacles

lifted it placing the sole of his boot firmly in the

ground neither stooping nor

*(She slices open the envelope. She removes the contents,
but does not unfold the page.)*

For such a man one word is

(She flings the letter and envelope back onto the tray.)

HANDKERCHIEF

I sometimes think she is not there

Things happen

Things occur but not always with that not always

with the satisfying sense of contingency

JEW

Oh I write grass and writes Jew

Tilted

Not violently but certainly a little inclined to the

left

The violence if it's anywhere is in the fact the

word is underlined

Once

For emphasis

I expect

DON'T BOTHER I'LL USE MY SLEEVE

That is the nearest I have ever come to sarcasm

Yes

But she's immune to it

Sarcasm is so cheap so self-defiling

NO I LIKE IT

IT'S ALL RIGHT I PREFER COLD TEA

Sarcasm again

I'LL TEAR MY OWN DRESS THANK YOU

Three times

I'm stopping there

Aristocrats are rarely given to sarcasm but a

Jew

She cannot help herself

(Pause.)

Possibly the word Jew

Standing

Solitary

On its own in the centre of the page

(Pause.)

Underlined but

(Pause.)

Underlined

(Pause.)

Underlined once only

(Pause.)

Could be read as an apology that is certainly
the way in which I intend to read it the word is
not dog after all if it were dog how different that
would be no no this word is an apology just as
the word grass is

(Pause.)

Placatory

(Pause.)
THAT IS HOW I HAVE READ IT IN THE
PAST
AND
WILL
CONTINUE
TO
AS
LONG
AS
Even the word dog let us be clear let us be brave
let us think where others fail to think yes
The word dog
On its own
Solitary
And even underlined
Would not
NOT NECESSARILY
Constitute
(Pause.)
Offence
(Pause.)
Oh no
Oh no
I like dogs
So do many
Dogs are also faithful
Dogs are also loyal
Teeth yes
And some are curs but
IT ISN'T SIMPLE IS IT
(Pause.)
How I hate simplicity its little laws its two and
two make four its black and white its tit for tat
its oh how loathsome always he writes Jew and

always I write grass how long can that continue
I don't know as long as it continues I suppose
excellent excellent excellent
THE STRANGE COMMUNICATION OF
DISTINGUISHED MINDS
Take
My
Note
NOW
NOW
NOW
I haven't licked the envelope
(She laughs.)
Now that's also
She's no fool
Also a routine
I shout
I make her hurry
Drop whatever she is doing
Ironing
Emptying the grates
Trip
Drop
Tumble
Hasten to obey
When all the time I have not sealed the
envelope
NO WONDER SHE IS SOMETIMES
DILATORY
I'LL LICK IT NOW
(Pause.)
What's that?
(Pause.)
Tongue out
Moisture

Strange action licking envelopes

Comic

Possibly absurd

An aristocrat she would lick her finger first and with the wetted finger travel down the gum but me I

(Pause.)

That sound what is it

(Pause.)

I understand perfectly well that both service and authority have limits to their obligations a mistress for example cannot expose her servant to dangers which for her own behaviour has

(Pause.)

AND YET SOME SERVANTS WOULD OH MAKE IT THEIR OWN HONOUR TO ENDURE EVERY

(Pause.)

I've read of them

Such servants

Yes

(Pause.)

Who perished for their mistresses because

(Pause.)

Because of the exquisite manner in which they sealed their envelopes

YES

YES

IT'S POSSIBLE

(Pause.)

I do not know that sound

(Pause.)

I do but

(Pause.)

It

(Pause.)

It

(Pause.)

I do not like a man to cry

(Pause.)

NO POSSIBLY THERE IS ONE YES A
SOLITARY JUSTIFICATION FOR MALE
TEARS ONE ONLY ONLY ONE

(Pause.)

Achilles failed the test of masculinity by weeping
for his lover anger yes and rage a man however
may weep only for his son

(Pause. The sound of weeping continues.)

Walked

Walked

As if in summer streets he saw a café with a
green tin table and passing between trams
dreamed a coffee dreamed a cigarette

STOP MY POOR MY POOR DO CEASE

(It continues…)

Oh my dear one the terrible the lake depth of
your grief shh shh

(Pause.)

Perhaps he also walked walked walked and did
not run and where he encountered obstacles he
also lifted

(Pause.)

I never knew you had a son an only son a
beloved and

(Pause.)

I never knew

*(The sound ceases. She is perfectly still. The sound of
distances and plains. A tray appears, laden with tea
things. It travels. Its pendulum movement slows to a
stop…)*

She's gone

My loyal but dilatory
Gone
My
Fled
My servant
To her parents in the woods he was a forester
and has a hut yes made of wood beech and the
roof is bark I saw it not the actual thing in a
photograph in a clearing where the sun drops
down in shafts just like a painting by that who
that oh my head that
RUYSDAEL
Father
or
The
Son
Jacob
Or
Solomon
(She puts a hand to the teapot.)
IT'S HOT
(She recoils. She laughs…)
This tea
Whilst it might be the thoughtful adieu of a loyal
servant however dilatory might also
(Pause.)
Always I jump to the wrong conclusions
(Pause.)
The better of the possible conclusions always
(Pause.)
It's in my nature
My nature prefers if only briefly to embrace the
kinder of the several interpretations in this case
to see the tea tray as a parting gesture but it's
wrong
(Pause.)

Quite wrong

Quite wrong

And a lapse of aristocracy because we oh it's the
most defining of all our qualities we are not

(Pause.)

Sentimental

(Pause.)

He sent the tray

OH ONE MUST LOOK INTO THE ABYSS

ONE MUST

ONE SPOILS OF SOMETHING IF

(Pause.)

One's gaze is forever averted

(Pause.)

He's sorry for me

He regrets

He has succumbed perhaps we all do in the end
perhaps we must it may be in the chemistry of
souls

Succumbed

To

Pity

(The bell rings.)

Now that

Oh

The Ineffable

(Pause.)

Refinement

(Pause.)

Of his ring

I'M WEEPING

I'M WEEPING

NOT FOR MYSELF

FOR HIM

I'LL GO

(She laughs at herself.)

I'll go I say I'll go as if another could she's gone
who else could go if anyone was going who else
but me

I'LL GO

That summons

Could anyone resist

It's a gesture

It's a token

It's a kiss

(The bell again, the same. She smiles.)

How subtle and how complicated I do not think
and this I do admire in a man I do not think he
fully understands himself is that not wonderful
that one so very oh so very

(Pause.)

Disciplined

(Pause.)

Should now proceed to issue signs which
contradict each other? First the tea, which if tea
means anything at all means patience, languor,
idleness, and then IT DOESN'T QUITE
MAKE SENSE DOES IT before I have had
time to pour let alone to raise the cup up to my
lips he rings it doesn't quite

(The same bell.)

There it goes again

Never have I disliked the fact of contradiction
rather I am charmed by it but in this instance

NO

NO

IT'S ALTOGETHER HIM

I don't object

I don't I'll pour in any case I'll pour as if he
were not in the least impatient and perhaps he's
not no this subtle ring is not impatience compare

it with the last that was that was impatience
perhaps he somewhat musically wishes to
accompany my drinking yes it's possible rather
as if the bell were what a violin yes
HE CANNOT SIT WITH ME BUT ALL THE
SAME DESIRES THAT HIS PRESENCE
SHOULD BE KNOWN

(It rings.)

You see

It's charming

Charming

I am

(She pours a cup of tea.)

Charmed

*(As she lifts the cup to her lips the sound of weeping
returns. She hesitates. She proceeds, attempting to
ignore it. A tray flies in, with the identical pendulum
motion to the last. As it passes before her eyes she
anxiously attempts to discern what it carries. The
contents of the tray are however concealed by a stained
cloth. The tray loses momentum, stops. At the same
time the weeping ceases. UND drinks, as if at leisure.
Then she thrusts the cup and saucer aside with a cry.)*

TAKE THIS AWAY

She's gone

She's gone

TAKE THIS AWAY

(She swings abruptly to the mirror.)

I don't look bad

My hair's gone white

I don't look bad

OUR IDYLL'S OVER

OUR POOR IDYLL

If it was an idyll

An idyll is what's over obviously

THAT WAS we say

UND

THAT WAS an idyll

(She laughs.)

He chooses to announce its termination by

Peculiar

Distinguished by peculiarity

His ways are recondite so very recondite

I don't pretend to understand

TAKE THIS AWAY

She's gone

TAKE THIS AWAY

(She weeps, recovers. Her hands go to the stained cloth. She swiftly removes them.)

No

No

I won't concede to this

How very gauche if I

HA…!

It's not for me to

AND HOW VERY UN

UN

UN

ARISTOCRATIC TO CONCEDE

(Pause.)

He's testing me

(Pause.)

Impertinent

(Pause.)

Amusing and impertinent

(Pause.)

To test the depths of my distinction he

Sends me a thing of utter and nauseous

corruption which if I lifted even the corner

would reveal me certainly to be

YES IT'S SHREWD

curious and common

I do think he is in his own way

(A deluge of sordid fluids pours from above which drenches her, horrifies her. She gasps. She struggles to regain herself. She extends her arms. She moans with self-disgust. She recovers a stillness. With infinite will she turns to face the mirror, unflinching…)

This man intends to murder me

(Pause.)

Walking

Walking

Fingers idly vertical as if in summer streets he saw a café with a green tin table and

(Pause. The gentle bell. She does not move. The bell coaxes her again…)

I'm not an aristocrat

I am a Jew

(She reaches for the edge of the sordid cloth on the tray. Her fingers remain suspended. The sweet bell again. She tears away the cloth. Her position at the mirror ensures she does not see what is revealed, nor does she attempt to.)

I'm not an aristocrat

I am a Jew

In my aspiration to authentic aristocracy I nevertheless exceeded all criteria for the thing called aristocracy

I was more

Yes

Vastly

More

Aristocratic than the

(Pause. She places her hands on the mirror frame and adjusts it in order to show what lies on the tray.)

Aristocracy

(Pause. The bell rings sweetly. A strange laugh comes from her. She releases the mirror, which swings on its

wires. A taut sound is emitted from a string. She goes to the yellow flowers on the tray and immerses herself in them. When she emerges the sound has gone.)

The last

The last and finest quality is this and I have

Me

More than anyone cultivated it

In me this quality has reached its apotheosis

I am describing

THE ELIMINATION OF SURPRISE

Me shocked

Me puzzled

Incredulity

Disbelief

No

Only that reflex of the nerves to sudden shock which no amount of moral education can eliminate no one who is still human who retains the characteristics of the species can for example refrain from jumping when a gun is fired next to the ear

That's nothing more than

That's mere

(Pause.)

Animal

(Pause.)

But jumping in the soul

(Pause.)

Never the aristocrat

(Pause.)

And never the Jew

(Suddenly she calls, and grabs up the flowers.)

PUT THEM IN A VASE

She isn't here

A VASE

She isn't here

THE VASE WHICH STOOD

She isn't here

NEVERTHELESS

(Her arm remains extended, clasping the flowers.)

Nevertheless

(A note. She struggles with her arm, refusing to concede to exhaustion. She stares at it as if it were not her own. She wills it to remain outstretched. She bites her lip with the agony of her persistence. She emits a smothered cry. She is at the point of collapse. A vase appears on a tray. She forgets her pain in the ecstasy of the vision. The pendulum goes to and fro and at last ceases. The vase is full of fresh water. She drops the bunched flowers in. She deliberately leaves her arm outstretched…)

Oh, how he loves me

(Her arm declines.)

What devotion

Reverence

And temper

He suffers for me

TO SIT OH NO

TO SHARE A TABLE OH ABSURD

AND THOSE EXQUISITE MANNERS

WHICH WE SHARE COULD ONLY

SEPARATE US FURTHER

(Pause.)

This is better

The betterness of this he knew

Yes

From the moment that my invitation touched his hand he knew

WE WERE MUCH TOO

OH TOO REFINED FOR ANYTHING BUT

(Pause.)

Suicide
(Pause.)
Suicide
The
Perfect
Truth
Of
Aristocracy
Is
Its
Contempt
For
Life

The air he walked through was not still but
shook with contrary winds small winds gusting
winds which plucked his tunic or pressed his
trousers flat against his hips and through these
winds perhaps the cause of them sailed bands
sailed hoops of tungsten razor sharp bowling
and bouncing sometimes colliding any one of
which could slice through flesh and bone divide
a man in half behead lop trim and singing
always singing this acquired a certain beauty so
he said and what was the horizon for want of a
better word the horizon rose and fell in constant
motion fountains geysers boiling plunging liquid
volatile and seen through tidal heat and rolling
clouds of toxins livid bile and copper green and
this acquired a certain beauty so he said into this
he walked walked walked he did not run and
where he encountered obstacles lifted his leg
placing the sole of his boot firmly in the ground
neither stooping nor attempting to present the
narrow profile of his body to the front his shirt
unbuttoned and wearing a soft cap not a helmet
in one hand a cane and in the other nothing

nothing nothing in the other hand but let hang
loosely fingers idly vertical as if

*(A sixth tray flies in. It swings before her. In her dread
of observing what it may contain, she closes her eyes.
Pause. The bell rings.)*

Yes

Yes

(The bell is insistent.)

Yes

(And again.)

I

Can

I

Will

(And again. She does not open her eyes.)

I will I said

(She does not look.)

Oh, listen

I do not wish to know how terrible you are

You rather

Need to know how terrible I am

*(He eyes open. Her eyes fall on the tray, now
stationary. A small heap of earth, freshly dug, is piled
on the tray. Pause.)*

Someone's dead

(Pause.)

Someone

(Pause.)

Someone's dead not me

(Pause.)

A little grave I saw him yawning in a café the
newspaper slipping from his hand and morning
this was morning sun streamed through the
curtain and his mouth was oh a cave and his hair
unwashed his face unshaven no collar marks of

dinner on his sleeve dark brows dark hair he's
dead this is his grave

*(She extends a finger and works it into the pile of
earth. She stops at the bottom.)*

Yes

Yes

IT'S HIM NOT ME

Pity

Pity

Flows from me

And graves like these they don't survive a winter
even under trees

In one pocket poems

In the other philosophy

The perfect perish why

IT'S A NECESSITY IT'S A VOCATION

(Pause.)

He will not ring again

IF HE DOES I'LL ANSWER IT

He won't however

DON'T YOU GO

She isn't here

She isn't here

IF HE DOES LEAVE IT TO ME

*(A pause. Her finger, dirty from the earth, is held
unconsciously. She discovers it. She examines it as if it
were not her own. As she does so a frame containing
a painting by Ruysdael drops beside the mirror…
Pause…)*

Solomon

Jacob

Solomon

Solomon

*(She observes the painting. Her finger remains erect. A
terrible hammering ensues. The hammering aquires a*

certain rhythm, a pulse, a music. UND does not move.
It stops.)
We
(It begins again, and continues. UND does not move.
At last it stops.)
We
(And again.)
We
(A new sound of dragging and friction.)
Distinguished by our aristocracy
The signs
The symbols
Oh the
Oh the
Delicacy of our forms
Oh
Oh-
I died on seeing
On seeing died
LET HIM IN
On
Seeing
Died
(It rains, steadily, heavily….)

THE TWELFTH BATTLE OF ISONZO

Characters

ISONZO
A Very Old Man

TENNA
A Very Young Woman

A blind bride seated.

TENNA: I'm marrying an old man
              (Pause.)
              Not rather old
              But very old
              Oh so very old this old man
              (Pause.)
              One rather old proposed to me
              But rather old is never old enough
              In rather old the young still shows
              Traces
              Fragments
              Archeology
              Very old is sightless
              Very old is weightless
              Skin
              Membrane
              Memory
              And humourless
              Of all youth's prejudices
              Of all youth's nauseating strategies
              Evasions
              Refuges
              The least forgivable is humour
              Whereas he
              Oh
              Not one syllable to deflect the pain
              Not a solitary irony
              Flung up to shield his sensibility
              (She lets out a cry.)
              And trembling
              (The same cry.)
              This trembling is not infirmity

He is so finely tuned
It is the world which plays his soul
A single string he vibrates to his agony
Shh
Oh
Shh
I am a winter
A winter of anticipation
Frost stiffens
My already stiff cunt hair
Ice cold my arse
And womb a solitary amphibian clings to my
floor
Mud deep
He
Only
Only he
Can thaw my
(The cry. She strains to hear. She cries again. Out of the following silence the sound of shuffling feet, which ceases, starts and ceases again.)
THE BRIDE WHAT IS SHE SOME WOULD
SAY THE GROTESQUE RELIC OF
ARCHAIC PRACTICES A TESTAMENT
TO MANKIND'S REVERENCE FOR
SYMBOLS WHICH RATIONALITY
LONG AGO CONSIGNED TO THE
SENTIMENTAL SPHERE THE REALM OF
APPEARANCES THE PREPOSTEROUS
BUT THERAPEUTIC SUBSTITUTION
OF PARODY FOR AUTHENTICITY I
HOWEVER
(She stops. In the silence, the shuffling feet, which cease.)
I KNOW THAT WHEREAS MARRIAGE
NOW AS ALWAYS BARELY CONCEALS
ITS MERCANTILE AND MATERIAL

TRANSACTIONS BENEATH A SPURIOUS
RHETORIC OF HARMONY THE BRIDE
(Her cry.)
SHE
(And again.)
SHE
THE BRIDE
SHE
(A pause. She is poised.)
Dine at my arse
And my piss
Go
Drunk
On
Out
(The shuffling feet precede the appearance of an old man, suited, blind. He is still like a bird, perched on two sticks. A pause.)

ISONZO: Infinite

My

Beauty

TENNA: Infinite

ISONZO: And I dreaded decay

TENNA: Briefly

ISONZO: Briefly I dreaded decay

TENNA: A misapprehension

ISONZO: A failure of nerve

TENNA: Not the first time

ISONZO: Not the first time I had experienced the failure of my nerve but briefly as you say I harbour one regret however only one that being blind you cannot speak my beauty in the normal way the normal way contemptible as it is having some residual value for me I have to say you cannot for example can you utter the immortal words

	SINCE I SET EYES ON HIM it hardly matters I merely felt the need to ventilate this scarcely detrimental irritation to my happiness the same applies to you of course
TENNA:	The same
ISONZO:	Exactly and having announced my irritation the irritation has evaporated
TENNA:	So often this
ISONZO:	So often
TENNA:	We discover this to be the case *(A pause. They are motionless.)*
ISONZO:	I hear your heart
TENNA:	Its
ISONZO:	Your kidneys
TENNA:	They
ISONZO:	The traffic of your bowel *(She crosses a leg over the other.)* Don't move Don't smother the streams and the cataracts of your landscape please Is it not the virtue of our sightlessness that we make no distinction any more between the surface and the depths your skin is like a bolt of silk thus far the sighted with their mundane metaphors but me oh me can I not say the wild warm liver of you shines like a porpoise in the bay
TENNA:	Yes
ISONZO:	Yes I saw bays once I saw porpoises you never did
TENNA:	Never Never saw a thing
ISONZO:	These bays were not distinguished These bays were never Naples Never Nice

	Nice came later
	Naples
	Nice
	Cadiz
	But we were poor
	I shan't describe it
	I shan't elaborate
	May I sit
	My knees are like confectionery
TENNA:	Perch yes
	Perch at my feet
ISONZO:	A bird
TENNA:	Bird heavy at my feet
ISONZO:	How wonderful the blind are in high heels

How wonderful their empty eyes blue shadowed
on the lids

Am I near

Am I

(He has not moved.)

I feel your warmth

The uncommon flavour of your breath

(He still has not moved.)

I'm proximate

I'm proximate

(Suddenly he flings down his sticks with a clatter. A pause elapses.)

TENNA: You have not fallen

(He is perfectly still.)

You have not fallen

(She emits a low laugh.)

How like you to

How superlatively you imitate the characteristics
of the senile

Their stratagems

Their policies

You have not fallen
You have merely cast away your sticks
You test me
Even at the altar
Test me
Is she fit to be my bride
Is she
Is she fit
And had I shrieked
A single gasp of spontaneous compassion
Slowly
Slowly
Your receding feet
(He laughs also.)
Yes
Yes
Abandoned at the very edge of matrimony
Yes
Listen
I am also wound more tightly than a spring
And now you must retrieve them
But how
How will you retrieve your sticks
Or stickless
You must crawl
Crawl if you wish
(ISONZO laughs.)
MEN HAVE
MEN DO
BOYS
WOMEN
Oh
Their extraordinary prostrations
Sheer extravagance
Through glass

Through shit
The deliquescence of cadavers
Yes
To reach my
Oh to reach
But not you
Crawling you decline to do
Not that you find crawling contemptible
If ever a man craved crawling
That man is you
But not where others have
In their small tracks
Impossible
I'm crossing this leg
Listen
Lifting this knee
I'll collect them shall I
Your sticks
Someone must
And if not me then

ISONZO: DON'T

TENNA: Who

ISONZO: DON'T
(TENNA laughs.)
Better I
However crippled
Better I
At God knows what hazard
Should grope towards

TENNA: Yes

ISONZO: My own salvation

TENNA: Yes

ISONZO: Than any other

TENNA: Yes

ISONZO: Should inflict their ruthless appetite for pity on
my defenceless flesh
I don't require the sticks
They were an affectation
(Pause.)

TENNA: You don't

ISONZO: No

TENNA: Don't require

ISONZO: No and never did

TENNA: Never required them

ISONZO: Never
But
Luxuriated
In
The
Peculiar
Authority
They
Lent
Me
(Pause.)

TENNA: Impossible
(Pause.)
Impossible
(Pause.)
YOUR WAR WOUND

ISONZO: A scratch
(Pause.)

TENNA: This alters everything

ISONZO: Everything?

TENNA: Not everything

ISONZO: Nothing at all

TENNA: SOMETHING IS ALTERED

ISONZO: What is altered

TENNA: Our passion

ISONZO: How

TENNA: Our passion

ISONZO: OUR PASSION NEVER WAS
            SUSCEPTIBLE TO TRUTH
            (Pause.)

TENNA: No
            (Pause.)
            No
            (Pause.)
            Collect the sticks however
            (ISONZO laughs.)

            For me also dissimulation is
            I'M TREMBLING

ISONZO: *(Who has not moved.)* Got them

TENNA: An ecstasy
            STICKS

            STICKS

ISONZO: Got them

TENNA: Old
            So old
            He hangs from sticks
            A rare epidiae
            In dusty museums
            Are fixed to pins
            Dry
            Desert dry
            And under glass
            (Pause.)
            Lie if you wish to
            Always lie
            And being lied to I
            Must wade through indignation
            Parting the membrane of my inhibition to admit

(She giggles.)

I'm wet between my legs
(Pause.)

So much for sticks
(She is suddenly afraid.)

You're blind

The blindness

OH THE BLINDNESS

THAT'S
(She shudders.)

ISONZO: Authentic

Yes
(Pause. He shuffles. He passes in front of her, laboriously. He stops. A pause.)

TENNA: I must

May I

Uncross my legs

ISONZO: SHH

TENNA: MUST

LET ME

UNCROSS MY LEGS
(He stifles his resentment. She uncrosses her legs.)

ISONZO: Odour
(Pause.)

Whilst I don't disparage it
(Pause.)

Odour
(Pause.)

And blindness made me a connoisseur I freely admit
(Pause.)

Odour has forfeited its

TENNA: AM I NOT SWEET

ISONZO: Its terrible imperatives

TENNA: OH SAY I'M SWEET

ISONZO: Its implacable authority over my instinct
YES YOU'RE SWEET
BUT STALE IS LUSCIOUS TOO

TENNA: Yes

ISONZO: STABLE STALE

TENNA: Yes

ISONZO: RIVER DEEP

TENNA: Yes
(Pause.)

ISONZO: Beyond the obligations owed to odour
The servility induced by sight
And touch with its subtle disciplines
There's rumour
I am now
In the final quarter of my life
IF IT IS FINAL
Addicted to the rumour

TENNA: Forgive me

ISONZO: Forgive you why

TENNA: Thinking you might
A man of your distinction might
Your subtlety
Your history might
Ha
Embarrassment
I'm blushing
Ha
Excruciating
Might
(She lets out her cry.)
Be gratified to know the fact of your proximity
has made me flow
(Pause.)

ISONZO: The rumour possesses this distinct advantage

(He suddenly emits a string of terrible cries, the depth of which doubles him.)

TENNA: *(Spontaneously rising to her feet.)*

Stop

Stop

Stop

Stop

(They cease simultaneously. TENNA's hand is outstretched but hangs in the air.)

You're dead

You're dead or dying

OH YOU HAVE NOT TOUCHED ME YET

(Pause.)

Or

(Pause.)

Given your contempt for touching

Consummated

In any form as yet

Our

Our

(She laughs a low laugh. Her hand remains in the air.)

ISONZO: *(Darkly.)* There'll be a form.

(Pause.)

TENNA: Yes

ISONZO: Oh yes

(He unbends, stiffly.)

A form exists for our

Believe me

(Sensing the proximity of her open palm. ISONZO cranes forward and rests his chin in her hand. TENNA shudders. ISONZO laughs. Then she laughs also.)

The war in which I was not wounded

That war in which it pleases you to think I was

The war I went to and returned from with a single scratch

Not deep

A scratch such as a child acquires from walking
in a forest

Or from a cat

This war has taken lodgings in my memory

And walks the attic floor

An undesired tenant

Eviction notices are pinned to its door

But still

You know memory

It comes back

Filthy

Vagrant

Bawling

At any hour of the night

I am a prisoner in my own apartment

Never mind

Never mind that
*(He is perfectly still. TENNA abruptly withdraws her
hand.)*

TENNA: I was not born then

Nor my mother either

And my grandmother in little frocks studied the
alphabet

ISONZO: I thought of her

TENNA: Green shutters

ISONZO: Studying the alphabet

TENNA: The storks rowing the blue sky overhead

ISONZO: I asked myself if studying the alphabet was
not precisely what had initiated all those many
actions which however random and unplanned
had cumulatively resulted in my lying naked in
a gas mask while parts of other men both known
and unknown to me rained from the sky brain

	teeth and viscera clots of arse and shards of thigh
TENNA:	The duck pond blue as love
ISONZO:	But on further reflection I was compelled to admit that if the alphabet had certainly contributed to my misery it was simultaneously the only means by which it could be alleviated
TENNA:	My grandmother
ISONZO:	Poetry and poison gas
TENNA:	My grandmother
ISONZO:	Their mutuality
	Their conjugality
TENNA:	My grandmother
ISONZO:	She was a little dear
TENNA:	Why naked
	You said naked
	Why
	(Pause.)
	Aren't soldiers clothed
	Aren't soldiers uniformed
	(He is resolutely silent.)
	Should I perhaps
	Oh
	Am I gauche
	Am I
	(Pause.)
	You must permit me to
	You must
	Throw open all your doors
	(Pause.)
ISONZO:	I'll try
	(She weeps.)
	I'll try
	(She smiles through her tears.)
	Obviously

I
Was
Clothed
OBVIOUSLY CLOTHED
THE COARSE BLUE CLOTH OF
BOOTS
OBVIOUSLY CLOTHED
(She is still with horror.)

TENNA: I'm crossing my legs
I'm crossing
Forgive me
Crossing my legs
(She swiftly uncrosses and replaces her leg across the other.)

ISONZO: I've been married

TENNA: Yes

ISONZO: Yes
I know the state
I know the obligations
MARRIED
AND
WITH
EYES
(Pause.)
Certainly the truth will come more easily this time
Marriage is proper only for the blind
(Pause.)
I said naked
Naked I said
Purely in order
Purely
Purely
To create an image worthy of the narrative
A naked youth

Naked in a helmet
Hermes
David
The Spartans at Thermopylae
THIS WAS MORE TERRIBLE THAN
THERMOPYLAE

TENNA:	Forgive me
ISONZO:	No
TENNA:	Forgive
ISONZO:	No
	Nothing to forgive
	I lied
	I lied to my bride
TENNA:	Do lie
ISONZO:	Thank you but
TENNA:	Lie my lover
ISONZO:	Yes
	Yes
	Certainly the habits of a lifetime are not easily
TENNA:	Oh lie
ISONZO:	On the other hand my wrists are weak
	(Pause.)
TENNA:	Your wrists
ISONZO:	Weak
	Yes
	A hundred years
	The serpent coiled around my thighs
	Its fangs
	Its yellow eyes
	A man grows tired
	(Pause.)
TENNA:	What serpent
ISONZO:	TRUTH

TRUTH'S A SERPENT

TENNA: Yes

ISONZO: Oh yes
A hundred years I've grappled
And now
Bloodless
Shrivelled
Dry
I am inclined to let it feed on me
Let it find what nourishment it can
BON APPETIT
SNAKE
(He laughs and stops.)
Describe your pants
(Pause.)

TENNA: Describe them
Why
When you can easily

ISONZO: The rumour

TENNA: Yes

ISONZO: The rumour
Always
The rumour
Please
(Pause.)

TENNA: I had a friend
(Pause.)
This friend
Whom I have now discarded

ISONZO: Why
(Pause.)

TENNA: Why
(Pause.)
You ask me why

(Pause.)

In order to be married
(Pause.)

That is why
(Pause.)

Hailing a taxi took me to the great department store at the meeting of eight boulevards

ISONZO: I know the store

TENNA: And leading me through glass and china shoes and leatherware manoeuvred me onto an escalator which rose to such a special silence I knew at once we had arrived in Heaven

ISONZO: I know the floor

TENNA: Six

ISONZO: Lingerie

TENNA: The Heaven of Unworn Underwear
(ISONZO laughs, stops.)
How beautiful anticipation is
How exquisite
How every garment murmurs its pathetic prayer
He placed my hand as if it were in pools of petals
Scented
Cool
And left me there

ISONZO: Tact

TENNA: He would not trespass

ISONZO: Oh tact

TENNA: He would not let his eyes intrude
Where I sifted for you one solitary and weightless pair

ISONZO: Shh

TENNA: Oh

ISONZO: Shh

(They dream.)
Shell pink
Shell pink
SHELL PINK
OR
IVORY
(TENNA laughs.)
What's funny

TENNA: I

ISONZO: What's funny

TENNA: I

ISONZO: Not funny I assure you

TENNA: I

ISONZO: GOD HELP YOU IF THEY'RE BLUE
(Pause. TENNA goes to cross her legs.)
Don't
(She freezes.)
Don't cross your legs
It's
This leg-crossing
Far from erotic
In this instance
Leg-crossing is anxiety
(Pause.)

TENNA: And my anxiety
Is that not
Erotic?
(Pause. He contemplates. Then with decision.)

ISONZO: Cross
Cross your legs
(TENNA completes the movement.)
I should have written
Or a friend
If I possessed one

Should have gone to you with two colours
written on a card
SHELL PINK
OR
IVORY
Your own friend
Now discarded
Could then have served us better
ARE THEY BLUE
Directing your slender fingers to the proper
place the place where only these two shades
could be discovered
RED EVEN MORE
OH
RED
I CANNOT SPEAK THE WORD
IT'S HERESY
IT'S SACRILEGE
Sometimes a single colour made me sick
Oh yes
Sick
On the counterpane over the curtains in the
very throat of her who gasping for my body had
exposed herself
GREEN FOR EXAMPLE EVEN NOW I
EVEN NOW
(He struggles with a compulsion to vomit.)

TENNA: *(Extending a hand into space.)* NOT GREEN

(A long pause. ISONZO finds a handkerchief. He wipes his mouth.)

ISONZO: Now this is interesting

TENNA: *(Intuitively.)* Yes

ISONZO: Most interesting because

TENNA: Oh yes

ISONZO: The blind

How brilliantly

TENNA: Oh yes

ISONZO: How terribly

(TENNA giggles.)

We might deceive

(Pause.)

It is perfectly possible your pants are

(Pause.)

Yes

(Pause.)

The very colour

AND YOUR BRA

(She shudders.)

The very colour

I find it impossible to speak

(He breathes with difficulty.)

I SAY IMPOSSIBLE OF COURSE I CAN I
CAN SAY GREEN GREEN FIELDS FOR
EXAMPLE GREEN BUS CATERPILLARS
CUCUMBERS

(Pause.)

Only in this solitary instance is the word so
certain to induce

(He stops.)

Oh

Oh

I think your underwear precisely is

(He shakes his head.)

The atmosphere between us

The little climate of this room

(He extends a tongue.)

Suddenly tastes of

Discreet

Untruth

CONFESS IT BITCH

CONFESS
SEA GREEN
LIME GREEN
MOSS GREEN
I'M BEING SICK

(His vomit turns to a spluttering laugh from which he slowly recovers.)

TENNA:	Interesting
ISONZO:	Yes
TENNA:	Most interesting because
ISONZO:	Oh yes
TENNA:	This unexpected
ISONZO:	Why
TENNA:	This unpredicted
ISONZO:	Why
TENNA:	Agony of colour
ISONZO:	WHAT'S UNPREDICTABLE ABOUT IT *(Pause.)*
TENNA:	*(Persisting.)* Is anyway Is surely Is Misapprehension *(Pause.)*
ISONZO:	Lie on *(Pause.)*
TENNA:	You do not know You cannot possibly KNOW IF I KNOW IDIOT *(Pause. Now it is he who giggles.)*

ISONZO: A blind girl going to her wedding fails to ask the one who dresses her the colour of her garments the crackling cellophane the subtle scents of unused items notwithstanding never even in the most cursory of ways lets slip a little curiosity as to the hue of those frail poems

POEMS

YES

She draws over her hips

Unlikely

Miss

Your lies are not yet in the major key

NOVICE

And do not call me idiot I am in love with you

(He shuffles nearer to her. She listens intently.)

The colour

Whether or not it is hypothesis

Cannot be allowed to cast a shadow on our lives

Remove them

Strip these pretexts for dissension from your flesh

TO WHICH THEY CLING

LIKE DROWNING MEN

(A long pause. She vibrates with tension.)

Are you

Are you doing it

(She moves with infinite delicacy, lifting her legs one after another. The sound of her stiff petticoats fills him with awe. He cranes his neck. He balances on his curiosity. Suddenly there is a clatter as she accidently unhooks a shoe in her movements. She freezes, one knee in the air, her pants in her hand. The pants are shell pink in colour. Pause.)

TENNA: These loved but

ISONZO: Shh

TENNA: Abandoned

ISONZO: Please

TENNA: I must speak

ISONZO: Please
(Pause.)
I know how hard it is
To be adored
To stand unflinching under scrutiny
As statues washed by fountains
(Pause.)
Thrive
On
My
Gaze
(Pause. He is still, the garment aloft.)

TENNA: Gaze?

ISONZO: I am a sponge

TENNA: Gaze?

ISONZO: Inhabiting the ocean floor and drinking
every element of your existence through
pores so sensitive as to be themselves hardly
distinguishable from the sea in which they
breathe
GAZE
OH YES
I SAY THE SPONGE GAZES
(Pause. He snatches the pants and stuffs them into a pocket.)
These eleven
Disparate
Varied
Both in colour
And in mood
Nevertheless had this in common

THE TWELFTH BATTLE OF ISONZO

A MARTYR'S APPETITE FOR TRUTH

Or

Or

Or

One must be strict even in recollection

MY BEAUTY INDUCED EVEN IN THOSE
UTTERLY CORRUPTED BY THEIR
FACILITY FOR LYING

A desolation such that they ached in this single
instance to lie not only naked but also

CLEAN

Does the bra match the pants

If so

(He touches something with a foot.)

Ah

The shoe

*(He sweeps the floor with a hand and plucks up
TENNA's shoe.)*

The bra must also be

Unhooked

Crushed in your palm

And flung into oblivion

Oblivion

Being

My

Trouser

Pocket

(He laughs. So does she…)

You are the twelfth

Don't break my heart

With honesty

TENNA: I am terrified of you

ISONZO: Good

TENNA: I suffocate

ISONZO: Good

TENNA: To think of you

ISONZO: Extend your foot

TENNA: On some bed breathing

ISONZO: Your foot I said

TENNA: Inches

Only

Inches

From

(He deftly replaces her shoe. She breathes audibly. He is perfectly still, his hand poised.)

How blind are you

How blind

(Pause.)

HOW BLIND I SAID

(She laughs a little.)

The bed on which we / if it is a bed / you will with infinite / or lawn perhaps / except it's winter / infinite tenderness / tilt me back / bed no / I do not think so / on reflection / so what if the lawn is thick with frost / tripping me gently with your heel / or summerhouse / bed may have comforted eleven / but the twelfth / no / silly / bed / never a bed / the shore of gravel pits / dense weed in railway yards / down in the mass of / sinking heels / down in / down in / mud / shale / splitting seed pods / rotting timber of the floor / stiff grass / grass fine as lightbulb glass / my arse bathed in a cold / my naked arse / the frosty lawn / I think the lawn for your first /

(A long pause.)

I cannot stay a rumour

(Pause.)

However perfect rumour is

(Pause.)

However the eleven

ISONZO: They weren't

TENNA: Rejoiced to be

ISONZO: There weren't I said

TENNA: Thrived on

ISONZO: NEVER RUMOURS THEM
(Pause.)

TENNA: Forgive me
My adolescence
My infant appetite
I ACHE TO BE

ISONZO: Ache
(She lifts her hands in a gesture of pain.)
As for the bra

TENNA: I am not wearing one
(Pause.)

ISONZO: Feel free to cross your legs
(TENNA instantly crosses her legs, a relief.)

TENNA: Eleven
Not so many when you think
Eleven
Taking your age into account
Advanced in age as you are
And the circles you have moved in
Is eleven very
No
The contrary
Eleven's few
I even
Even I
At seventeen
Have
I don't say this to
Or perhaps I do
To torture you

DO I SAY THIS TO TORTURE YOU

	Have loved four times
	(A long pause.)
ISONZO:	Name them
	(A long pause.)
	Name
	These
TENNA:	No
ISONZO:	These
TENNA:	No
ISONZO:	Mundane clerks and lawyers
TEN :	Not clerks
ISONZO:	Guitarists
	Singers
	Students of art
TENNA:	Not guitarists
ISONZO:	Who breathed the clichés of desire in your infant ear
TENNA:	Or singers either
ISONZO:	Who smeared you with looted sentiments of literature and film
	Name them
	Name
	The
	Derivationists
	Who plucked your soul
	Bitch
	(Pause.)
TENNA:	Later
	Later I will name them
	Or rather
	Given them names
	(She laughs out loud.)
ISONZO:	Excellent

TENNA:	Naked
ISONZO:	Excellent
TENNA:	Naked
	Only
	Naked
	Could
	I
	Utter
	Them
	As if by wading through my womb you stirred a flock
	Scattered a shoal
	Shook out of hibernation rodents which panicking fled
	By my mouth
	Never
	To
	Return
	(A long pause.)
ISONZO:	Oh
	Oh
	Did
	Anyone
	Did
	Ever
	Anyone
	Place more of their life's hope in this one act
	Than
	You?
	(Pause.)
TENNA:	Only you
	(Pause.)
ISONZO:	Only me
	(Pause.)

UNDRESS I HAVE TO SEE YOU NAKED
UNDRESS UNDRESS

Oh

Bride

What's bride but the apotheosis of delay
(TENNA reaches for her left shoe.)

Shoes last
(She freezes.)

I think
(She remains still.)

Don't you?
(Pause.)

Emerging from the seething finery / the foam
of / surf of / breaking and cascading seas of
starched and pleated / tucked and pinned / oh
don't ask me / tied / beribboned / oh don't ask
me / white bodiced / binding white / you step /
still whiter /
(Pause.)

But still in shoes surely?
(Pause.)

I've seen the films
(Pause.)

It is obligatory
(TENNA stands.)

OH GOD
(He shudders.)

Your standing

Your rising to your height

The swirl

The whispers of your

Murmurs

Odours

Rivers

Straw

MY HEART VAULTED

From one side to the other
(He trembles. He places a hand on his heart.)

TENNA: Dare I
(Pause.)
Given your frailty
(Pause.)
Dare I
Lift
Even
One
Hem
Now?
(ISONZO hears his heart.)

ISONZO: It's swinging
On two arteries
As if a child called by its mother
Flung himself
From off a creaking swing
(TENNA is in terror.)
Risk it
Inflict your nakedness on me
(She is poised, hesitant.)
Inflict I said
(She contemplates him. His face tilts, searches.)
That's not
(Pause.)
As I have understood it
(Pause.)
Even a sketch of nakedness
(Pause. At last she reaches for the zip which fastens her gown at the back. She draws it down, stops.)
Go on
(TENNA does not proceed. ISONZO laughs.)
Yes
Yes
How right to set the pace yourself

ELEVEN TIMES I SET THE PACE
ELEVEN TIMES MISTAKEN
Yes
Yes
Adored one
Yes
(A long pause. TENNA does nothing. ISONZO grows uncomfortable.)
On the other hand
(TENNA shakes her clothing without however exposing herself further. A pause.)
Now wait a minute
(She laughs a low laugh.)
Yes
Exquisite
Exquisite trickery
I KNOW
I KNOW

TENNA: HOW DO YOU KNOW WHEN YOU CAN'T SEE
(Pause.)

ISONZO: Blood

TENNA: Blood?

ISONZO: Blood flows faster in the naked obviously
(He cackles.)
NAKEDNESS
IT'S NOT JUST NO CLOTHES IS IT

TENNA: No

ISONZO: IT'S PAIN
IT'S FEAR
IT'S HORROR
(Pause.)
So the blood flows faster

TENNA: Yes

	And you
ISONZO:	Hear everything
	The music of the veins
	Just as before
	I heard the cascades of your vulva
	As one hears plumbing in an empty house
	(Pause.)
	Proceed
	(Pause.)
	Oh
	(He chuckles.)
	Now I smell the sweetest odour of resentment
	coming out of you
TENNA:	Yes
	(Pause.)
	Everything you say is true
	My fear
	And my resentment at the fact my fear is known
	to you
	(Suddenly TENNA is seized as if by a fit. ISONZO lifts his hands to discover her.)
ISONZO:	WHAT
	WHAT NOW
	(TENNA fights for breath.)
	WHERE
	PLEASE CAN WE JUST
	(He senses catastrophe.)
	Beloved
	(He staggers.)
	Adored
	(She gasps.)
	Oh angel
	Oh
	Impossible that you should
	(She is silent, still on the chair.)
	Has she predeceased me

Pre

De

Ceased

The word is too

Oh too familiar to me

ALL ELEVEN

PRE

DE

CEASED

ME

Yes

I kept a check

TENNA: *(Recovering.)* I haven't

ISONZO: Not this time

TENNA: Not this time no

I merely

I

Since childhood I

This tendency to

Asthma

ISONZO: Asthma

TENNA: Low blood pressure

ISONZO: The pressure of your blood is low

TEN: And this inclines me to

ISONZO: Carry on now
(Pause.)

TENNA: Carry on?

ISONZO: Undressing
(Pause.)
Carry on with it
(Pause.)
Your medical biography is frankly
And the schools
The habits of your parents

Favourite authors
Dominating influences
Frankly
Hold
No
Interest
(Pause.)
Later possibly in some drowsy aftermath
of ecstasy the drone of your unexceptional
confessions might
(TENNA laughs.)
Soothe me as water or birdsong completes the
polyphony of idle afternoons
(And laughs.)
Now however
(Pause.)

TENNA: Now I must be naked
(Pause.)

ISONZO: It's inevitable
(Pause.)

TENNA: Yes
(Pause.)
And what's inevitable
(Pause.)
Once conceded to

ISONZO: BRINGS RELIEF
(TENNA lifts her hands to her straps. A tension suffuses her. She slips the straps off her shoulders. The room is plunged in darkness. In the ensuing silence, the sound of her short breath. Then a terrible wail comes from ISONZO.)
CAN'T
SEE
(Pause.)
NAKED
AND

CAN'T
SEE
(Pause.)
Oh did I hope
Oh did I dream the shock would punch the sight
back into my eyes as falling masonry I've heard
bricks cabinets or tiles have on exceptional
occasions brought vision to the lifelong blind
AND THIS IS EXCEPTIONAL

How old are you

TENNA: How old

ISONZO: Your age

TENNA: You know my age

ISONZO: SPEAK IT ALL THE SAME

TENNA: I'm seventeen

ISONZO: SEVENTEEN

Oh I call that exceptional
NAKED AND SEVENTEEN
(Pause.)
How proper I am blind
I never could have looked upon you cleanly
Not cleanly
Only through encrusted lenses lenses smeared
with grief and scored by ludicrous transactions
shame-dim guilt-splashed fissured by monotony
*(He laughs. A slow dim light spreads across the naked
buttocks of TENNA. ISONZO removes his glasses.)*
I'm not blind
(Pause.)
I merely shut my eyes
(She is utterly still.)
And you are perfect
(He moves closer.)
Funny word
Perfect

Funny
Funny
Word
Now we have dispensed with God
With Paradise
And in my own case so it seems
With Death
We can say perfect
WHO DARES CONTRADICT US
(Pause.)
I'm not blind and the proof is this

TENNA: DON'T SAY
(Pause.)
Don't say
My arse
My arse will know if you are blind
From your first kiss
(Pause.)
It won't betray you
(Pause. ISONZO is still.)
Kiss
(Pause.)
Do kiss
(Pause.)
Do kiss or I'll think
(Pause.)
I'LL THINK A MILLION THINGS
(Pause.)
You've left the room
You've left the room for some and I'm
(Pause.)
YOU HAVE NOT LEFT THE ROOM
(Pause. She resorts to sarcasm.)
It's nice
I don't mind this

Naked

NAKED AND ALONE

Lovely

Lonely

Nakedness

(Pause.)

I think you are

Forgive me

Stretching the pleasures of anticipation to their
breaking point

ELEVEN RATHER ANGRY WOMEN I
DARESAY

(Pause. He is still.)

Oh

Find

The

Panic

Of

Your

Adolescence

I'm

Cold

(ISONZO only observes.)

And I thought he will swallow me

So perfect me he'll take the hot brine from
between my thighs

He'll bathe

He'll swim

So perfect me

He'll fasten to my fundament

So perfect me

Mouth to my mouths

Drink

Taste

All that flows fast or travels slow

The clean
The unclean
Abolished in me
I'M COLD
I'M COLD
(She goes to drag the wedding gown over herself.)

ISONZO: Stay naked
(Her hand freezes, clasping the fabrics.)

TENNA: Why
(She wails.)
Why
(Pause.)

ISONZO: Because I have to suffer you
THIS IS NOT COPULATION
I'M NOT A DOG
(He erupts into laughter. TENNA sobs.)
I said that
The selfsame words
As she
Don't ask me which
More open to me than a dawn
More fluid for me than an oyster
One of that eleven
Found my procrastination more than she could
bear
FETCH A DOG THEN
Oh
Oh
Divine riposte
(He shakes his head.)
And dogs could educate me
Possibly
(Pause.)
Mother nature
What

A
Prig
Is
She
What
A
School
Miss
Always
I
Skipped
Her
Classes
A
Prince
Of
Truancy
Caned
Caned
Obviously
FETCH A DOG THEN
(He laughs. A long pause.)

TENNA: Of the eleven
Of them
The discarded and deceased
Were any
(Pause.)
Was even one
(Pause.)
One even
(ISONZO laughs low and complacent.)

ISONZO: Not one
Consummated
No

(A brief, profound silence. A horror seizes TENNA. She drags up her clothing, tight to her chin.)

Oh

Adieu

To

Nakedness . . . !

TENNA: *(Smarting.)* I

ISONZO: NAKEDNESS

TENNA: I

ISONZO: WHAT IS IT AFTER ALL

TENNA: Oh I

ISONZO: WHAT IS IT BUT ANOTHER
          DOWN PAYMENT ON A DEAL?
          (Pause.)

TENNA: *(Resolutely.)* I cannot lie beneath your gaze

ISONZO: My gaze?

TENNA: If that gaze

ISONZO: What do you know about gazes?

TENNA: That gaze is

ISONZO: You're blind

TENNA: A GAZE WHICH NEVER HAS
          IN ALL THOSE YEARS
          NEVER
          NEVER
          (She is lost for words.)
          I DON'T KNOW
          OH GOD
          IT'S HORRIBLE
          (She sobs. She turns away, the fabrics still taut over her.)
          I pity them
          I pity me
          Gazed upon
          A landscape
          A picture in a gallery

GAZED ON BUT NEVER SEIZED
(She recovers.)
Any man who looks on me
MUST
RAGE
AND
RIP
THE
AIR
WITH
HIS
IMPATIENCE
(ISONZO declines to reply.)
All twelve of us
Reduced to
Rendered into
IMAGINE IF YOU CAN THE DEPTHS OF
OUR HUMILIATION
(Pause.)
Of course you can imagine
Humiliation is precisely your intention
I've heard of this
A friend
Or possibly a novel
Yes
A memoir of the eighteenth century
In braille
A narrative of broken women
RAPE IS BETTER
YES
BETTER TO BE VIOLATED THAN
(She gropes the air. Her hands fall.)
Appetite
Frankly
Is

Preferable

Oh

Yes

Thank God

For

Appetite
(She laughs, lightly, gaily.)

Speak then
(Pause.)

Say something
(He is still.)

Oh

How

We

Hated

That
(Pause.)

All twelve of us

That silence

ARROGANCE

NOT

SHAME

Offend me more

Add

Add

To injury
(Still he declines to speak… She shakes her head.)

And now I sound like them

I sound precisely as they sounded

Horrible

But then my cries of ecstasy

Had such cries existed

Might well have imitated theirs

Pleasure or complaint

The same old notes

The same old instrument
I FAILED THE TEST
(She releases the tight hold on her clothing.)
Not your test
If you set tests
THE TEST I SET MYSELF
(Pause.)
Did I
(She lifts a hand in disbelief.)
Did I select a man of such
Oh ludicrous
Such age and such distinction
In order that he should in absolute conformity
with all men young and old distinguished and
undistinguished
SIMPLY FUCK
(She spits her contempt.)
No
There were eleven
And these eleven were
SODDEN WITH CONVENTIONALITY
Then came a twelfth and she
(Pause.)
She
(Pause.)
Was
(Pause.)
Blessed with this
(Pause.)
Infinite capacity for
(Pause.)
Abstraction
(A long pause. She is proud, erect…)

ISONZO: How exquisitely you indict yourself and I am
not a virgin
(Pause.)

How wonderfully you swing from rage to
absolute accommodation my tired body lay
in dockland brothels nights on end Durazzo
Genoa and Kiel but mostly Kiel so often Kiel
when I was not a sailor one might investigate the
strange pre-eminence of Kiel not only brothels
either palaces sham Gothic sham Baroque and
once a tram depot the driver's little boots she
knew oh how she knew the power of her little
boots her service was the last off went the lights
the watchman slammed the great doors of the
shed Olmutz that was why was I in Olmutz
(Pause.)

I'm pole hard
(Pause.)

Pole hard for you
(Pause.)

TENNA: And is that
(Pause.)

Are we to
(Pause.)

I DON'T KNOW ANYTHING WITH YOU
(Pause.)

Should one deduce from this
POLE HARDNESS
Any
Any
Oh silly but
I'M YOUNG AND NEVER WAS IN
OLMUTZ
Any outcome?
(She falters.)
POLE HARD NO OBLIGATIONS
(She turns swiftly.)
NOR DITCH WET NEITHER
How we have triumphed over Genoa and Kiel
(She laughs.)

The swift

The spontaneous

The unreflecting

Poverty of fornication

NOT FOR US

ISONZO: POLE HARD

TENNA: Instead we are submerged in contemplation

ISONZO: POLE HARD

TENNA: As two aborted foetuses bottled for the medical museum stare at one another through the glass

ISONZO: POLE HARD

TENNA: *(Bitterly.)* STOP SAYING POLE HARD

POLE HARD FOR WHAT

WHAT IS THIS PITIFUL POLE

HARDNESS?

(Pause.)

ISONZO: A promise written in the air

(Pause.)

TENNA: *(Charmed.)* Yes

(She springs up, drawing up her knees.)

Yes

You a promise

Me a rumour

Immaculate suspension

Perfect poise

Oh

How gross

How coarse

How concrete

PROXIMITY WOULD BE

I SHOULD SHRINK

(She thrusts out a hand.)

Where are you

Where

(She gropes.)

A hand

A solitary hand

Please

(Her hand is outstretched. ISONZO shuffles near. He lifts his hand. Their fingers touch. Suddenly TENNA withdraws her hand and clasping her gown to her, struts about.)

Alone among the twelve I

Lavished with blindness

Lavished with youth

I

Only I

Can reach beyond the

No

Not reach

VAULT

VAULT THE TURBID POOL OF

INTIMACY THAT SWAMPS OUR PATH

Its clays

Its sediments

Its clinging

(She stops suddenly.)

I've travelled

Oh

How travelled I am

And now I don't mind being naked

(She lets her clothing fall.)

Nakedness

Oh

What's nakedness

It's being without

(Pause.)

Clothes

(She is relaxed, her limbs move easily as she returns to the chair. Her fingers discover it. She sits. She tilts back her head. She bounces her foot loosely. A long pause.)

ISONZO: They all said that

TENNA: THEY DID NOT

THEY DID NOT SAY THAT

ISONZO: In fewer words

TENNA: THEY DID NOT

THEY COULD NOT POSSIBLY

ISONZO: In less exquisite words

TENNA: IN NO WORDS AT ALL

LIAR

HYPOCRITE

LIAR

(She ceases. Her foot still bounces.)

ISONZO: And that's the agony of age

(Pause. The foot bounces.)

Not sickness

Infirmity

Decay

But this

As if one ran down corridors

This

And every room was

Every one

THE SAME

CRASH

The door flung back on its hinges

Groping for the light switch

The chandeliers aflame

Or blinds racing to unleash the day

PRECISELY

THE

SAME

FURNITURE
PRECISELY
THE
SAME
FABRIC
PRECISELY
THE
SAME
(Pause.)
I have outlived the world
The poor poor world
Poor you'll find it
Or possibly
You know how I applaud your sensibility
This poverty
Is already
Known to you?
(A long pause.)

TENNA: What an extraordinary life we two have had
(Pause.)
All that two might do
Done
Or if not done
So thoroughly pondered
That doing
Could only fail to do what doing promises
(She laughs.)
DOING OH
DOING'S FOR THE DIM
I'll kneel for you
To be precise
BESTRIDE YOUR CHEEKS
These cheeks are charts charts of your ecstasies
Winds off estuaries
Smoke of battles

Perfumes smudged from sordid and unsordid
Rouged from smacks
Varnished by restaurants
Adolescent blushes
Senile razor scars
My unblemished thighs
No birth blood
No sparkling stream of semen ever
Travelled down
Lie
Prone
Prone
Now
I'm
Perfect
And
A
Bride
(Pause.)

ISONZO: Prone
Ha
The world
Always
The world
Wanted me prone
Shrapnel
Liquor
Women edging their arses to my

TENNA: BE PRONE I SAID
OH
DO
BE
PRONE
(He ponders.)

ISONZO: Prone?

But

Prone's the

Prone's

TENNA: Yes

ISONZO: DEATH
(He goes down like a dropped sack.)

TENNA: *(As if panicked.)* Where are you

Where

Where

Are

You

Prone?

(ISONZO is silent. The naked TENNA picks her way over the floor. Her extended shoe touches his body. She lowers herself over ISONZO, feeling his features with the tips of her fingers. She is still.)

The beauty of the widow what is it the grief surely the depths of grief which by common consent cannot be plumbed the depths of solitude impossible to cross and yet the beauty of the widow what is it she staggers in her sleeplessness dark hollows where her eyes the shrunken lips and yet what can console her nothing nothing can console her and yet and yet
(Pause. She slaps his face.)

RAGE

RAGE AT YOUR LOSS
(He is silent.)

Against some cemetery tree a yew a yew tree yes the sodden odours of the clay blind monuments some hammer in the distant docks lifting her clothes he tearing at her clothes he all hands all garments could not find her here she guide me here she said her cry made rooks lift off
(Pause. She slaps him again.)

RAGE
RAGE AT YOUR LOSS
(Pause.)

ISONZO: But I've done that too
(TENNA frowns.)

TENNA: Done that?

ISONZO: In Lisbon
Yes
Lisbon it was
I could not find her
Here she said
I fumbled
WHERE
HERE
WHERE I SAID
(He laughs.)
She would not guide me
She declined to
The widow
Declined to guide me
Obviously
What's a widow
What's a widow
NOT A WHORE
No
The
Onus
Was
On
Me
Explore she whispered
Oh, explore
I was impatient
Shh
Explore

	No rooks however
	Rooks in Lisbon
	Few and far between
	(Pause.)
TENNA:	And I
	At your funeral
	Inconsolate
	Shall I
	I also be
ISONZO:	OH YES
	OH YES
	ALWAYS
	ALWAYS ANOTHER ME
TENNA:	Don't say that
ISONZO:	Oh
TENNA:	Don't say another you
ISONZO:	Every minute
TENNA:	Don't
ISONZO:	ANOTHER
	FLOPS
	ONTO
	THE
	MATTRESS
	(Pause.)
	Or the stubble
	Some
	After all
	Are
	Born
	In
	Fields
	(Pause. Tears stream down TENNA's face.)
	You cannot
	Oh

You cannot bear to contemplate
The sheerly
ORDINARY
Nature of all things
At 17
NOR COULD I
(She heaves with sobbing.)
Suffocate me
Make this kiss the last
(Pause. She goes to remove her dark glasses and stoops to kiss ISONZO.)
No
(She stops.)
Kiss
Me
With
Your
Arse
(She hesitates, the glasses aloft.)
In
That
Rank
Foliage
I'll
Squirm
A
Little
(She is quite still.)
In
That
Lush
Undergrowth
Warm
Pools
Will

(She is motionless.)
Drown
An
(Pause.)
Inquisitive
(Pause.)
Child
(TENNA seems poised to accede to ISONZO's request, but stops suddenly.)
What
What
WHAT'S THE

TENNA: Shh

ISONZO: Shh why

TENNA: *(Fascinated, removing herself from him.)* Shh I said

ISONZO: *(Frustrated in his aim.)* I'M ON THE
THRESHOLD OF OBLIVION
(In the silence, the distant sound of a wedding carillon, brought on a wind. TENNA listens with rapt attention.)

TENNA: Oh, I so require to be...
(She sobs.)
A BRIDE MUST BE OBSERVED
(As the carillon swells in volume, TENNA is drawn to the sound. Inspired, ISONZO, unable to rise off the floor, kicks his legs like a doll. TENNA blindly collides with one thing after another in her attempt to leave the room. The bells stop. TENNA's hand goes to her face.)
Nose bleeding
(Pause. She extends her hand in the air.)
Nose bleeding
(ISONZO does not reply.)

12 ENCOUNTERS WITH A PRODIGY

Characters

KISSTER
a Boy of 12

COLOGNE
his Governess

TOLEDO
his Tutor

TUESDAY
his Friend

SAMUELLA
his Mother

GABRIELE
his Ecstasy

BEHEMOND
a Vagrant

GNASH
a Female Vagrant

MARSTON
a Thinker

MENDEL
Father of Gabriele

RAGSIT
a Victim of Plague

SCHOCK
Father of Tuesday

TERESA
Mother of Tuesday

OLMUTZ
an Angel

PRESSBURG
an Angel

CANNAY
a Mortuary Assistant

RILEY
a Lover

I

A child rehearses.

KISSTER: I was born at a roadside. Planes swooped
overhead, firing cannon. Five uncles died, three
of them clutching clocks. These clocks chimed
as in their last convulsions my uncles crushed
them to their chests. The fields were barley.
When the barley burned it gave off dense clouds
of smoke. This smoke attracted the attention of
looters, rapists, and psychopaths. For two days
my mother hid me in a drain, lifting the iron lid
to feed me and replacing it again. For two days
she was subjected to unspeakable barbarities.
Her body was the site of more refined depravity
with every passing hour. To this day she bears
the scars of –
YES –
YES –
The scars of her ordeal not only on her body but
also in the deepest –
OH –
OH –
RECESSES –
RECESSES of her mind, hardly a night goes
by without the darkness tearing like a sheet as in
some nightmare she dives and screams, I force
the pillow tight around my ears and –
I'm not going on –
I'm stopping there –
Don't make me –
I WON'T –
I WON'T –
*(He sits defiantly on the floor, his legs stuck out in
front of him... A woman emerges from the shadows...*

she regards him with exasperation…his eyes at last rise to meet hers…)

COLOGNE: You are such a such a such a clever child –

KISSTER: I know –

COLOGNE: Such a clever child –

KISSTER: Yes –

COLOGNE: And it –

KISSTER: I know –

COLOGNE: WOUNDS ME SOMEWHERE IN MY –

KISSTER: I know –

COLOGNE: IN MY MOST TENDER PLACE THAT YOU WILL TIP YOUR LIFE LIKE WATER DOWN THE SLUICE –

KISSTER: Yes –

COLOGNE: BECAUSE YOU WILL NOT CONCEN-TRATE…!

(She is suddenly calm, collected. She moves to and fro with the patient demeanour of a gifted teacher…)

What is the first law of human behaviour Kisster?

KISSTER: Coercion.

COLOGNE: And how does coercion announce itself?

KISSTER: By violence.

COLOGNE: Only by violence?

KISSTER: No. It has a number of masks.

COLOGNE: Name the masks of coercion, Kisster.

KISSTER: Pity. Argument. And Shame.

COLOGNE: And which is the greatest of these?

KISSTER: Pity. Can I play now I have been indoors for –

COLOGNE: No –

KISSTER: Indoors for two hours –

COLOGNE: WHY NOT WHY NOT INDOORS FOR A HUNDRED HOURS –

(He smarts.)

KISSTER, I AM SAVING YOUR LIFE…!

KISSTER: I know, I know –

(He sobs… COLOGNE goes to him, kneels, hugs him to her…they rock in one another's arms…)

COLOGNE: You are so clever, so very, very clever –

KISSTER: *(Stifled.)* Mmm –

COLOGNE: And I adore you –

KISSTER: Mmm –

COLOGNE: Adore you with the vehemence of a perverse maternity whose –

KISSTER: Mmm –

COLOGNE: Is without –
(She kisses him powerfully on the lips…)
Perimeters –
(She thrusts him away, and scrambles to her feet.)
AND SHAMELESS SHAMELESS KISSTER…!

KISSTER: *(Wiping his mouth.)* Yes…
(She stares at him… Pause.)

COLOGNE: You do not want to play…you have no more desire to go outside and kick balls in gutters than I have to jostle fat women at market stalls…the sun is hateful to you…look how pale you are and when your hands are dirty you frown as if some vile excrement had been smeared on a sacred robe –

KISSTER: I LIKE FOOTBALL…!

COLOGNE: Oh, lie, lie, Kisster, it delights me –

KISSTER: *(Stamping a foot.)* LIKE IT I SAID…
(Pause… She examines him…coolly…)

COLOGNE: Yes…
Yes…
And I am the one who is so soddened with her inconsistencies…! Me…! For if my kisses did not make you squirm how repellent this would be…! I require you to exhibit all the signs of an offended modesty…recoiling and drawing your hand across your mouth as if… I were…as if my kiss…
(He goes swiftly to her and thrusts his hand into her skirt. She draws backward.)
No…!

Beast…!

No…!

(He desists. She laughs, resting her hands on her knees… Pause…)

Rehearse your birth. Word perfect and I. With that tenderness of terrible confession and then I. For each time that it's told it must possess the quality of revelation and not be anecdotal. Then I. My black centre. I. Kisster.

(She bites her lip, peering at KISSTER…he begins his speech.)

KISSTER: I was born at a roadside.

II

TOLEDO: *(A blind man.)* Is he there the little bishop surely the swish of his long linen on the tiles surely the slap of sandles progress progress we the outcasts we the world's slow oozing tide of indigence creep to your feet progress progress…!

(KISSTER walks up and down.)

Listen he is walking on our hands our fingers are a brittle path ow snap we fracture we disintegrate and faces bloom with purple hues of pain ow snap but silent who would dare let suffering past his teeth ow snap

(KISSTER walks up and down.)

Go –o– od…!

Go –o– od…!

Thy stricken sprigs of sodomy thy tumours of intransigent impetuosity lie heaped lie sprawled lie airlessly corrupting where his infant ankles tread fluid from our veins

Wash…!

Wash…!

(He rolls onto his back.)

Wash in that fountain of warm waters my –

KISSTER:	No –
TOLEDO:	Encrusted and uptilted face –
KISSTER:	No –
TOLEDO:	Lif – ted –
	Lif – ted –
KISSTER:	I AM NOT PISSING ON YOU –
TOLEDO:	Lif – ted –
	Face…
	(He proffers his face. KISSTER ignores him.)
	Cur.
	Vermin.
	Cur.
KISSTER:	Yes.
TOLEDO:	You have no feelings.
KISSTER:	I do have feelings and –
TOLEDO:	Reptile.
	Rodent.
	Reptile.
KISSTER:	My feelings tell me –
TOLEDO:	Please…
	(A long pause.)
KISSTER:	I do not know if – refusing you what you so desperately crave – I am protecting myself from an act I have no desire to perform, or – completely indifferent as to whether I perform it or not, I am simply enjoying your despair…
TOLEDO:	It is despair…
KISSTER:	Yes…
TOLEDO:	Please…
KISSTER:	No.
	(He puts a finger to his mouth…)
	And it would be so easy to –
TOLEDO:	NOTHING
	EASIER
	NOTHING
KISSTER:	To –
TOLEDO:	Please –
KISSTER:	To –

TOLEDO:	Please –
	(Pause. KISSTER seems about to relent.)
KISSTER:	Is that the point, however? Is the ease with which an action might be –
TOLEDO:	YOU BASTARD PLEASE –
KISSTER:	Performed sufficient reason for –
TOLEDO:	I'M BLIND…
	(Pause.)
KISSTER:	Yes –
	(Pause.)
	You're blind so I –
TOLEDO:	IT'S AN OBLIGATION, KISSTER.
	(Pause.)
KISSTER:	Open your mouth…
	(TOLEDO obeys.)
	Wider…! I might miss…!
TOLEDO:	Miss by all means…!
	(He extends his face… KISSTER steals from the room, leaving TOLEDO on his knees, abject, pitiful. After some seconds, the sound of a football kicked against a wall. Deducing his condition, TOLEDO's mouth closes into an agonized fence of teeth. A second youth skips in, sees TOLEDO, guesses his dilemma.)
TUESDAY:	Shall I –
TOLEDO:	Shall you…?
	(An awkward pause…)
TUESDAY:	Do what – whatever you –
TOLEDO:	Not the same if you – whatever I…
TUESDAY:	No, but –
TOLEDO:	Not the same at all whatever-I-with-you…
	(TUESDAY shrugs…)
TUESDAY:	Please yourself…!
TOLEDO:	I will, thank you…
	(He climbs to his feet.)
	I am a romantic you see… I have a wholly irrational predilection for the –
	STOP THAT FOOTBALL
	I LOATHE FOOTBALL

THE VERY SCOURGE OF THE
ENQUIRING MIND
An inextinguishable spirit of discrimination
which cause me to –
THAT BALL KILLS ME
KILLS ME
KISSTER *(Pause.)*
(It ceases... Pause.)
What else is discernment but a form of love...?
ALRIGHT, DO IT –

TUESDAY: What –
TOLEDO: Now...! Quick... Oh, God...!
*(He kneels, his hand reaches violently for TUESDAY,
who nimbly skips aside.)*
I'M BLIND...!
*(His hand hangs in the air, a mute appeal. TUESDAY
studies him. He returns. His hand goes to his fly.
TOLEDO presents his face... TUESDAY is about
to urinate on TOLEDO when he becomes aware of
KISSTER in the door, a football under his arm... A
long pause.)*
Oh, flood...!
Oh, flood...!
(Pause... TUESDAY's eyes rest on KISSTER.)
The bitter fermentation of your infant rage...!
WASH...!
WASH...!
*(His hopes fade... His head drops... He gathers his
coats around him and climbs to his feet.)*
So little to ask...
So impossible to acquire...
Mischief you would think – mischief alone –
contempt even –

TUESDAY: It's Kisster –
TOLEDO: Or cruelty –
TUESDAY: Kisster stopped me –
TOLEDO: The whooping savagery of infantile malevolence –
TUESDAY: IT'S KISSTER I SAID... *(Pause.)*

TOLEDO: Yes…

TUESDAY: Looking at me…

TOLEDO: Yes… *(Pause.)*
Kisster prefers my agony to his own delight…
surely in Kisster we discern the rudiments of a
novel consciousness…one might perhaps…were
it less painful…rejoice to be the subject of his
first contemplations…unfortunately, one cannot
avoid the suspicion he intends to make the
entire world squirm on the rack of his –

KISSTER: *(Moving in at last.)* You are a thoroughly bad
teacher and if I pissed in your mouth once I
should have to piss in it again. Soon you would
become bored with my pissing on you and
almost certainly I should have to smother you in
shit. Before long this too would cease to gratify
you and in next to no time I should find myself
sliced into pieces and spread about the town in
paper bags, the subject of an exhaustive police
inquiry and –

TOLEDO: PRUDE
Cur
Rodent
And
PRUDE
How I loved to teach teaching was my ecstasy
but you have single-handedly crushed every
pleasure in the little fist of your insouciance
STOP
BOUNCING
THAT
BALL…

KISSTER: *(Catching the ball.)* Yes.
Yes… Football in for me… I must confess…
(He kicks the ball violently away.)
An affectation… I merely wished to demonstrate
my mastery of some absurd activity…which I in
any case…held in contempt…

(He looks to TUESDAY*…)*
You may have the ball, if you can find it, I shan't
kick a ball again…

TUESDAY: *(Aghast.)* Kisster –

KISSTER: Yes, it went over there somewhere –

TOLEDO: *(As* TUESDAY *dashes out.)* COME BACK…!

KISSTER: *(Following* TUESDAY's *movements.)* It's in the
nettles… Still, he goes wading in… Ouch…!
Ouch, he goes…! *(He calls, points.)* To the
right…! *(To* TOLEDO.*)* Not really, I just like
seeing him – *(Pointing again.)* FURTHER…!
Ouch…! HIS FACE IS A KALEIDOSCOPE
OF AGONY AND GREED… Ouch…!
Ouch…! I wish, oh, I do wish you could see…
(TOLEDO's hand is irresistibly drawn to KISSTER's
knee… It hesitates.)
TO THE LEFT, NOW…!
(He laughs with a simple, infectious delight…
TOLEDO *touches him.)*
As soon as he recovers it I shall insist he gives
it back…! And he will…! Dear Tuesday, he is
infinitely forgiving… THE WORSE YOU ARE
THE MORE HE…
*(TOLEDO exposes and worships… His pleasure is
complete when* TUESDAY *enters with the ball…*
TOLEDO *is so swift to his feet that nothing is evident
to* TUESDAY, *who rubs his arms and knees.)*

TUESDAY: I was stung…

TOLEDO: You were stung…! Then you have had an
education in relative values which I, for all
my powers of elucidation, could never have
imparted so efficiently…take out your books…!

TUESDAY: *(Removing a worn book from a pocket.)*
Kisster, I mustn't have the ball…

TOLEDO: Remind me of the page… Kisster…
*(*KISSTER *is still.)*
Tuesday…

TUESDAY: Thirty-one…

TOLEDO: Page thirty-one…

TUESDAY: I mustn't have the ball…

TOLEDO: Thirty-one is the story of the pigs. Read, Kisster.
            (Pause… KISSTER is immobile.)
            Tuesday…

TUESDAY: *(Reading.)* 'Circe came down to the –'
            *(He stops, seeing TOLEDO has suddenly drawn up
            his legs, forced his elbows into his sides, and is mutely
            enduring a spasm or fit which causes his spectacles
            to drop to the floor… TUESDAY stands, horrified…
            KISSTER, whilst aware of TOLEDO's ordeal, remains
            seated, looking vaguely into the distance.)*
            Kisster…
            (TOLEDO drops off his chair, writhes on the floor.)
            KISSTER…!
            *(Strange sounds issue from TOLEDO as he grapples
            with a mortal blow… KISSTER turns to look at the
            spectacle.)*
            DON'T JUST SIT THERE WHEN –
            *(TUESDAY rushes to strike KISSTER, who catches
            his arm by the wrist. They grapple, knocking over
            the chair…they fall, their combat as desperate as
            TOLEDO's own…they roll across the floor… A flock
            of starlings passes, shrill… TUESDAY, more powerful
            than KISSTER, straddles him and beats him about the
            face… TOLEDO dies, still at last… TUESDAY ceases
            also…he climbs off his friend…he looks at TOLEDO's
            body…)*
            Kisster… Toledo's dead…
            (KISSTER is perfectly still.)
            Kisster –

KISSTER: Pick up the chairs.
            *(For want of a better thing to do, TUESDAY stands the
            chairs on their legs.)*

TUESDAY: I think dead, do you…?

KISSTER: Never strike me again…

TUESDAY: His eyes are all –

KISSTER: You are not to strike me

NOT MY FACE
NOR ANY PART OF ME

TUESDAY:	Kisster –
KISSTER:	Because my feelings don't accord with yours.
TUESDAY:	No –
KISSTER:	Help me up –
TUESDAY:	Help you up…?
KISSTER:	Yes –

(He holds out an arm… TUESDAY looks at him for the first time, tearing his eyes from TOLEDO's face…)

TUESDAY: It isn't you that needs help, Kisster –

KISSTER: *(Insistent.)* Help…

(TUESDAY goes to KISSTER, lifts him by the hand… KISSTER looks at TOLEDO.)

Mr Toledo was a bad teacher but in retrospect we may be obliged to say that, compared to other teachers, he was less bad than at first appeared. We shall encounter many worse than him, I feel sure, and whilst it is true that he pestered us with his insatiable appetite for urine –

(TUESDAY laughs.)

He did not – let us be just at this sad moment in the history of the world – *(TUESDAY laughs again.)*

He did not COERCE us into spilling it over him – *(TUESDAY is choking.)*

He only pleaded, whined and groaned, whereas –

TUESDAY: *(Shaking.)* Kisster –

KISSTER: Others will, I feel certain, bawl at us, throw us to the floor, and threaten us with death if we do not co-operate in acts far worse –

(TUESDAY is reduced to whooping.)

So all in all –

(He begins to laugh himself.)

He was A DEAR…!

(They both choke…shudder, their hands hanging by their sides…they gulp…recover…)

TUESDAY: Co – erce…what's co – erce…? *(Pause.)*

KISSTER: It's – *(He shrugs.)*
           Beating people round the face, Tuesday…
           *(TUESDAY is crestfallen… A pause… KISSTER's face
           suddenly crumples.)*
           POOR TOLEDO…!
           POOR TOL – EDO…!
           *(He weeps, gasping, torrenting, and gasping again…
           TUESDAY watches, horrified.)*

III

SAMUELLA: *(Entering in furs.)* How is it here?
           *(Pause. She looks at KISSTER…he seems lost for
           words…a long pause.)*
KISSTER: Well – *(He cannot speak.)*
SAMUELLA: And the room is pleasant enough warm enough
           what a nice view it has and your own wash-basin
           do you like the room the bedspread has little
           pictures of Paris on it perhaps a little feminine
           say and it can be changed what's wrong with
           feminine things anyway it might make boys
           nicer to have dolls about instead of all this
           football all this army all this and she is kind to
           you she listens to you children are not listened
           to enough they are capable of extraordinary
           perception children extraordinary suffering I
           was myself I was oh so… *(Pause.)*
KISSTER: Yes… *(Pause.)*
SAMUELLA: How handsome you are one day you will drive
           a woman mad I say a woman I mean several
           hundreds possibly completely mad they say
           good looks are not the only thing I disagree of
           course an ugly character is worse than an ugly
           body I suppose I don't know where is sex where
           does it happen I ask myself but good looks help
           you say something or I just ramble I find the

	way you look at me embarrassing and when I am embarrassed I resort to –

way you look at me embarrassing and when I
am embarrassed I resort to –
(Pause…she bites her lip.)

KISSTER: You see, I don't believe you are my sister…

SAMUELLA: Really, not your sister, what am I then…!
(He is silent. He observes her.)
Not your sister…! I think you spend so many
hours on your own and these outlandish books
give you ideas not that I disagree with reading
books are wonderful at your age I devoured
books I knew the works of all the authors I say
all the ones that mattered twice or three times
some of them –

KISSTER: I was born at a roadside. Planes swooped
overhead.
(SAMUELLA observes him, frowning.)
You pretend to be my sister but who does that
help?
(Pause.)

SAMUELLA: I'm not sure…who it helps…
(Pause.)

KISSTER: And that is so often the nature of a lie. Not
that I object to lies, I think some lies are very
beautiful. But they perish rather quickly, like the
blossom of night-fragrant plants…
(Pause.)
So one might say – without embarrassment or
shame – this lie – this particular lie – has rotted
away…
(She stares…she crosses a leg…she looks at the floor.)

SAMUELLA: You are handsome and very clever also…
(He watches her.)

KISSTER: Let me see you without clothes…
(She half-shrugs, half-smiles.)

SAMUELLA: No…

KISSTER: But you want me to…!
(She stares…he looks at the floor…)

There can be one reason only for you denying
me the sight of your naked body.
(He looks up.)
You are my mother…
(Pause.)

SAMUELLA: You were born at a roadside, you just said…
KISSTER: Yes, but to whom…?
(Pause.)
SAMUELLA: I am delighted with my life…
KISSTER: Good…
SAMUELLA: I have a wealthy husband whose vulgarity is not
dissimilar to my own…
KISSTER: Yes…
SAMUELLA: Nothing would induce me to hazard what I have
so carefully –
KISSTER: Nothing, no…
(Pause.)
SAMUELLA: Shall I lie down…
KISSTER: Yes, lie down…!
(She lies on the floor. She loosens her clothes.)
Do you think of me often…?
SAMUELLA: No…
KISSTER: No…!
*(He laughs…he stares…she unbuttons…her eyes on
the ceiling…her hands come away, stretch, are still.)*
I was born at a roadside. Planes swooped
overhead, firing cannon. Five uncles died, three
of them clutching clocks…
SAMUELLA: Poor boy…
(He is drawn nearer.)
You are not to kiss me…
KISSTER: *(His lips on her naked flesh.)* No…
These clocks chimed as in their last convulsions
my uncles crushed them to their chests…
SAMUELLA: You are absolutely not to enter me –
KISSTER: No –
(He explores her.)

The fields were barley. When the barley burned it gave off dense smoke…
(He kisses her.)
The smoke attracted the attention of looters, rapists, and psychopaths…
(And covers her with his body.)
For two days my mother hid me…in a drain…

SAMUELLA: A drain…?

KISSTER: A drain…!

SAMUELLA: Oh, poor, helpless infant – no…!

KISSTER: Lifting the iron lid…and replacing it again…

SAMUELLA: Kisster…you are –

KISSTER: For two days she was subjected to…
(Even as he insinuates himself between SAMUELLA's thighs, KISSTER is aware of a figure who has entered and observes…he lifts his head and meets the eyes of COLOGNE.)
Subjected to…

SAMUELLA: To what…? To what was she subjected…?
(The absolute stillness of COLOGNE is interpreted as approval… Pause.)

KISSTER: Unspeakable barbarities…her body…

SAMUELLA: Go on…go on…!

KISSTER: The site of…
(SAMUELLA draws KISSTER tightly to her, stroking his head with a profound compassion…he weeps… SAMUELLA also…even as they make love…which, ended, becomes lighter, bemused… Pause.)
Who was my father, then…?

SAMUELLA: *(Sitting up.)* I couldn't say…shoes…!

KISSTER: *(Collecting up her shoes.)* Couldn't say…?

SAMUELLA: Shoes…!

KISSTER: I'm getting your shoes, they're –

SAMUELLA: And if you want new wallpaper, tell Miss Cologne, say –
(He extends a shoe. She squirms into it.)
Say you don't like views of Paris, you would prefer pictures of aeroplanes –

KISSTER: It isn't the wallpaper that has views of –

SAMUELLA: Everything is paid for –

KISSTER: I know –

SAMUELLA: By the wealthy husband whose vulgarity is not dissimilar to my own –
(She kisses him, hurriedly, is about to go…but stops.)
I don't know that…
(She waves a hand.)
After this we need – ever to meet again – do you…?
(Pause.)
Let's call it quits…
(Pause.)

KISSTER: What…? Call what quits…?
(She looks at him…he boldly returns her look.)
Yes…
Yes…
(She turns smartly to leave.)
I do think –
I do think –
Naked you were wonderful…
(She smiles.)
But dressed you are so vile…
(She looks at the floor…she goes out smartly.)

COLOGNE: You are such a clever child…such a…such a clever child…one does not know how to begin to comfort you…for fear you will…despise even the words that comfort comes in…
(He shrugs.)

KISSTER: Oh…
(He takes aimless steps…stops.)

COLOGNE: Find your football and –

KISSTER: No.
(Pause. He looks at COLOGNE.)
I think I should wash –

COLOGNE: Yes –

KISSTER: Bathe –

COLOGNE: Yes –

KISSTER: *(A sudden frown.)* Or not? Bathe or not?
(COLOGNE is puzzled.)
Perhaps her…
Possibly her…

COLOGNE: Bathe, yes –

KISSTER: Her fluid on my body…

COLOGNE: Wash it off –

KISSTER: Is holy –

COLOGNE: Holy –

KISSTER: MY SISTER…! How could I have a sister like that? If I had a sister, she would be as silent as a book…
(Pause.)
Wouldn't she…? She would not talk, my sister, because she would be unafraid of me. She would not froth. No, I shan't wash.

COLOGNE: Very well.

KISSTER: Let it linger…

COLOGNE: Yes –

KISSTER: Let it cling…

COLOGNE: As you wish –

KISSTER: It is my body…

COLOGNE: It is your body, yes.

KISSTER: *(With a paroxysm of pain.)* I FIND THEM DIFFICULT, BODIES –

COLOGNE: Yes –

KISSTER: Difficult…!

COLOGNE: *(Reaching out a hand.)* Yes, oh, yes…

KISSTER: VERY HOLY EVEN IF SHE…HERSELF…
(He shrugs.)
Is vulgar…
(He takes the proffered hand. He smiles…)
Yes…
Yes…
I find no contradiction in ascribing holiness to an individual who in every word and action bruises, wounds and damages our sensibility, no, holiness is elsewhere, holiness is not discernible

in the way that, for example, generosity or
cruelty is, no, I find no difficultly in – let's walk –
(He leads her.)
in placing holiness among those categories which
defy the normal terms of moral evaluation –
(He looks up.)
It's Autumn…! Though I have only seen – or
to be more accurate – been present at – eleven
Autumns – still I feel the onset of this season as –

IV

GABRIELE: *(A child of 12.)* these woods are private.
(She blocks their path.)
For centuries my family have lived here.
This long residence confers rights as well as
obligations. For example, we clear paths and cut
timber. We remove dead tress and plant new
ones.

COLOGNE: It is a beautiful place. We love to wander here.

GABRIELE: Of course it is beautiful… It is beautiful because
we make it so. Do you think it could be beautiful
on its own? Go back the way you came or I will
whistle a dog.

COLOGNE: Perhaps this beauty should be shared with
others?

GABRIELE: Why? Have you cleared the paths? Have you
dug ditches? I have never seen you.

COLOGNE: We are simply walking –

GABRIELE: SIMPLY WALKING…! My family did not
plant these woods for you to simply walk in.
(Pause.)

COLOGNE: Then who did they –

GABRIELE: For me to simply walk in.
(Pause.)

COLOGNE: You are not a very kind young girl –

GABRIELE: No, but I must have the woods to myself. If I
            have the woods to myself I am free. If I share
            the woods with you, I am not free. How simple
            that is…!
COLOGNE: Free to –
GABRIELE: I do not have to argue with you. When you have
            dogs, you need not argue. That must be why my
            father has so many dogs.
            (Pause… COLOGNE looks steadily at the girl.)
COLOGNE: You are very pretty and rather cruel.
GABRIELE: But also I am free…! Which is far nicer than
            either prettiness or cruelty.
            (Pause.)
KISSTER: I will tie you to a tree and the dogs will bite you
            cunt.
COLOGNE: Kisster…
GABRIELE: Will they?
COLOGNE: Kisster was born by a roadside…
GABRIELE: I can believe it –
COLOGNE: Planes swooped overhead firing canon…
GABRIELE: So what?
KISSTER: Whistle the dogs…!
GABRIELE: I will whistle them when I am ready…
COLOGNE: Five of his uncles died –
GABRIELE: I am not the least bit interested in his uncles –
KISSTER: The dogs will run home to your father, baying,
            bits of your panties dangling from their mouths –
COLOGNE: Kisster…
GABRIELE: Will they…?
KISSTER: Whistle the dogs…!
GABRIELE: I will whistle them when I am ready and not to
            please you –
KISSTER: Your father will run, horrified, into the woods
            and see you strapped against the tree, blood
            running and the hounds dragging out your
            womb…
            *(GABRIELE stares at KISSTER, unafraid, curious…
            KISSTER is black with rage, biting his lip.)*

GABRIELE: Perhaps the dogs are you…? Perhaps it's you that wants to bite my womb…? Are you a dog, Kisster? *(To COLOGNE.)* Is he a dog, your boy?

COLOGNE: Walk your woods in solitude, we will find another place.

GABRIELE: What sort of dog?

COLOGNE: Some light. Some air. This canopy of trees I find oppressive –

GABRIELE: Here, boy…! Here…!
(With a swift and supple movement, GABRIELE steps out of her pants and tosses them to KISSTER, whose hand instinctively goes out. He fails to catch them. They fall to the ground…pause…then he bends to retrieve them.)
No…! *(He stops.)*
Not in your hand, silly. Your teeth…!

COLOGNE: *(Extending a commanding hand.)* Kisster–
(A turbid pause… KISSTER goes down on his knees.)
Kisster…!
(And takes up the pants in his teeth. GABRIELE is amused, surprised.)

GABRIELE: Good boy…!
(She slaps her thigh.)
Here, boy…!

COLOGNE: Kisster…
(KISSTER growls. He crawls towards GABRIELE… who extends a hand to the pants and a second to stroke KISSTER's head. His jaws remain locked…)

GABRIELE: Let go…
(He is adamant.)
Let go…
(She turns to COLOGNE.)
Your dog I think requires a beating…
STICK…!
(COLOGNE, enraged, glares at GABRIELE.)

COLOGNE: It is you who needs the beating…! Kisster, get up you are –

GABRIELE: Stick…!

(She casts about for a fallen twig or branch.)

COLOGNE: Making such an idiot of yourself –

GABRIELE: Stick…!

(He growls at COLOGNE…she stares.)

COLOGNE: Get up or I will beat you myself…

(He growls. Swiftly, COLOGNE unbuckles her belt and draws it through the loops of her skirt.)

How dare you…!

(He growls again. COLOGNE straps him…he howls… in a bitter rage she strikes him again. GABRIELE, bemused, and now in possession of a stick, laughs out loud.)

GABRIELE: My turn…!

COLOGNE: *(To GABRIELE.)* Don't dare strike him, you repellent little land-owner…!

(To KISSTER.) Kisster –

GABRIELE: You are not hitting him hard enough –

COLOGNE: Kisster –

GABRIELE: I know all about dogs –

COLOGNE: Let go of those pants –

GABRIELE: I'll hit him –

COLOGNE: YOU DISGUSTING PIG…!

GABRIELE: *(Laying in.)* He is not a pig he is a dog –

COLOGNE: DON'T HIT HIM I SAID –

(KISSTER howls… GABRIELE laughs.)

SPIT OUT THOSE PANTS…

(She thrashes, GABRIELE brings down the stick.)

SPIT…!

SPIT…!

(KISSTER is beaten from two sides. Howls and then more human sounds come from his thrashed body. Only exhaustion causes the women to stop. From a distance, the authentic barking of dogs, aroused…the women stand uncomfortably. KISSTER sobs with pain. He rolls onto his back, the pants still in his mouth.)

GABRIELE: I must go home for dinner…

COLOGNE: All right, go home…

GABRIELE: I've lots of pants…

COLOGNE: Have you? Good…
           (She does not move…pause.)
GABRIELE: I'll go straight up to my room. No one will know.
COLOGNE: Put on clean things.
GABRIELE: Yes…
           (She remains still…pause.)
           Do you think he loves me, or is it just…
           (She shrugs.)
COLOGNE: I couldn't say…
           (Pause.)
GABRIELE: I think love is the most likely explanation…
COLOGNE: Do you…?
GABRIELE: Yes.
COLOGNE: Well, if you are so certain –
GABRIELE: Love of a rather hopeless kind. Futile adoration.
           Adolescent and –
           *(COLOGNE kisses GABRIELE on the mouth, the power
           of her kiss driving GABRIELE backwards some paces.
           The kiss ends. COLOGNE is breathless, shaken by the
           exertion of it. GABRIELE wipes her mouth.)*
           You see I am not free…!
           (She stamps her foot.)
           Diana roamed the woods in order to be free…!
           She did not roam the cities, did she? She did not
           walk the streets…! (She turns.) I am here every
           day but not Wednesdays I have lessons then.
           *(She runs away. The sound of dogs leaping and
           barking. The sound fades. KISSTER has not moved…
           COLOGNE also remains quite still, as if in shock.
           At last KISSTER jumps up, plucking the pants from
           between his teeth and tossing them to the floor.)*
KISSTER: You strapped me.
COLOGNE: Yes.
KISSTER: What is the first law of human behaviour,
           Cologne?
COLOGNE: Coercion, Kisster.
KISSTER: And how does coercion announce itself,
           Cologne?

COLOGNE: By violence, but you asked for it…! *(She bites her lip.)*
Lying on the floor… I was embarrassed…

KISSTER: Perhaps you envied me. Perhaps you wished to take her pants into your mouth, Cologne? Perhaps you could not bear to see her pants in mine?

COLOGNE: I don't know –

KISSTER: You don't know…?

COLOGNE: All right, I do know, yes, I love her, I hardly know her but I love her, I love her madly and I – *(She goes to snatch up the pants from the ground, but KISSTER is quicker. He sweeps them up.)*

KISSTER: No…!

COLOGNE: I LOVE HER GIVE THEM TO ME –

KISSTER: No –

COLOGNE: GIVE THEM TO ME YOU VILE BOY…! *(He taunts her.)*
Keep them, I don't care. What do I want her underclothes for? *(He tosses them to her. She catches them. She tucks them into her clothing. Her eyes remain on him, defiantly.)*

V

BEHEMOND: You again.

KISSTER: Me and you are even filthier than yesterday.

BEHEMOND: It rained.

KISSTER: It rained but what you require is to be flung into a river.

BEHEMOND: That might do it.

KISSTER: A raging river, swollen by storms, so that as you bobbed along your flesh was scraped on walls and tree trunks and your hair combed out by gratings, spikes and drains…

BEHEMOND: *(Laying a chess board.)* White or black?

KISSTER: White, I the spotless boy must be white and you
              the filthy tramp, black, obviously.

BEHEMOND: Try black for a change.

KISSTER: I don't like change. If I liked change I should not
              persist in playing chess with you. Should I?

BEHEMOND: You are your own worst enemy.

KISSTER: I shan't live long…

BEHEMOND: Good.

KISSTER: I have already contemplated suicide…

BEHEMOND: Don't draw the line at contemplation…

KISSTER: It is possible that the single reason I refrain from
              suicide is the desire to beat you at chess.

BEHEMOND: I must contrive to lose…

KISSTER: *(Opening the game.)* White pawn to King Two…

BEHEMOND: Same old opening.

KISSTER: Exactly.

BEHEMOND: I have never encountered a child of such leaden
              inflexibility…
              (He moves a piece.)

KISSTER: Nor I a tramp who stank so vilely, I am moving
              my chair –
              (He shifts the board and chair.)

BEHEMOND: The joy of infancy surely is its freedom from
              habit, its immunity from routine? Only instinct,
              temper or sheer whimsicality should govern its
              actions and command its will –

KISSTER: *(Moving a piece.)* King's Knight to Queen
              Three…

BEHEMOND: Yesterday's game…! I pity you…!

KISSTER: Identical, and everything you say is mundane
              and conventional.

BEHEMOND: Don't stay…

KISSTER: Where is the virtue in vagrancy if it fails to shake
              the edifice of your intellectual complacency?
              (He moves a piece.)
              You stink, but to what end?

BEHEMOND: *(Moving a piece.)* Check.

KISSTER: *(Moving his own piece.)* When I am a vagrant – as
I fully expect to be –
(BEHEMOND scoffs.)
And stink and limp and ooze from incurable
sores –

BEHEMOND: *(Another move.)* Check.

KISSTER: I shall expect this vile regime of poverty to at
least instruct me in –
(KISSTER makes a move, taking BEHEMOND's piece.)
Rare and extraordinary opinion, arrived at
through the deprivations of –
*(BEHEMOND sends the chess board flying in a clumsy
imitation of an accident. The pieces roll over the
ground. Pause.)*

BEHEMOND: Whoops…
(A long pause. KISSTER looks at BEHEMOND.)

KISSTER: I was winning…
(BEHEMOND stares back.)
Wasn't I?
(Pause.)
Winning…?
(BEHEMOND just stares.)
And you –
(He laughs…his eyes meet BEHEMOND's.)
Pick up the pieces, you scum.
(Their eyes stay locked… Pause.)
Get on your knees and retrieve the pieces,
scum…

BEHEMOND: You are putting your life at hazard…

KISSTER: Is that so, the bishop's in the gutter…
*(He does not take his eyes from BEHEMOND…his arm
indicates the chess piece.)*

BEHEMOND: I will strangle you and fill your mouth with
pawns…

KISSTER: And the black queen's there…

BEHEMOND: She can be stuffed in your arse…

KISSTER: Scum, kneel in the road and collect the pieces…
(Their eyes remain fixed.)

BEHEMOND: *(With decision, he gathers up the scattered chessmen.)*
If I killed you –
KISSTER: If –
BEHEMOND: If, obviously, if –
KISSTER: If I permitted myself to be killed –
BEHEMOND: *(Grovelling and gathering.)* If you did, or if I took
you wholly by surprise –
KISSTER: Not possible –
BEHEMOND: Are you saying there is no such thing as
surprise…!
(He stops, on his knees.)
Are you seriously proposing that surprise – the
thing surprise – the category – has no place in
your cosmology –
KISSTER: No, I have been surprised –
BEHEMOND: *(Collecting again.)* Excellent, you have
experienced surprise –
KISSTER: I could not be surprised by you…
(Again BEHEMOND stops… Pause.)
BEHEMOND: Kisster…
(He shakes his head.)
I beg you to retract that statement…
KISSTER: Beg, by all means…
BEHEMOND: I do, I do beg…
(He is still. KISSTER looks at him.)
You wish me to say that what I know to be the
case is not the case?
BEHEMOND: *(Pause. His head hangs.)* Always, you make things
worse…
(He stands.)
I shan't play chess with you again…
KISSTER: Very well.
BEHEMOND: *(Bitterly.)* And I have so – so – so enjoyed your
company…
KISSTER: *(Folding up the board.)* This only confirms you
inability to surprise me, Behemond…
BEHEMOND: You should be killed…! You should be…!
KISSTER: Why? Because I will not genuflect before your –

BEHEMOND: To save the world from pain.
          (Pause… KISSTER looks down, bites his lip.)
KISSTER: Perhaps the world deserves the pain…that I shall give it….?
          (Pause. BEHEMOND shakes his head and starts to go.)
          Don't got, Behemond…you scum…don't go…
          (He drifts away… TUESDAY scampers in and flings himself in the empty chair.)
TUESDAY: Who won…?
KISSTER: Me, of course…
TUESDAY: You…! You never win…! Why do you say of course…?
KISSTER: Because of course it was inevitable I would win one day. It was a matter of time, that's all. And having won once, I should have won every game thereafter.
          (He smiles at TUESDAY.)
          Behemond knew that…silly scum…pick up the pieces, Tuesday…
          (TUESDAY unreflectingly gathers up the last chessmen, placing them on the table. As he finishes, he stands up the fallen chair BEHEMOND had occupied.)
TUESDAY: I can't see you again… *(Pause.)*
KISSTER: You neither…! Why?
TUESDAY: My father says so.
KISSTER: Oh, ignore your father.
TUESDAY: How I should like to…!
KISSTER: Come here tomorrow.
TUESDAY: I can't.
KISSTER: Tomorrow at this time.
TUESDAY: No.
KISSTER: Do as you're told…!
          (TUESDAY looks at KISSTER, level.)
TUESDAY: You see, my father says you order me about…
KISSTER: Yes, but you like to be ordered about. There's no shame in it. Tell your father that you and I have complimentary characters –
TUESDAY: *(Laughing.)* What…!

KISSTER: Com – plim – entary char –act – ers… *(Pause.)*
             Tell him we are like – *(He ponders.)*
             Like – *(He shrugs.)*
             A lock and a key…
TUESDAY: A lock and a key…?
KISSTER: Is the lock inferior to the key? Is the key
             subordinate to the lock?
TUESDAY: I don't know…!
KISSTER: Of course neither is superior to the other. They
             merely fit. Tell him that.
TUESDAY: *(Smiling.)* Yes…
             (Pause.)
             No, he won't listen to that –
KISSTER: I'll write to him.
TUESDAY: He won't read it and anyway you do boss me
             and I can't come tomorrow my father's right he
             always is I don't think we shall ever meet again
             except in class and you skip class so even then
             it's…
             (KISSTER stares into the distance.)
             Kisster…
KISSTER: Be here tomorrow or I shall seduce your mother
             and kiss her in between her legs.
             (Pause… TUESDAY's face is wrinkled.)
             I am an orphan…
TUESDAY: Yes… you were born by a roadside, I know…
KISSTER: There you are, then…
TUESDAY: Yes…
             (Pause.)
KISSTER: Tomorrow.
             *(TUESDAY is in agony. KISSTER does not glance in his
             direction. TUESDAY runs out.)*

VI

GNASH:	Too many enemies…
KISSTER:	*(Standing and launching the box of chessmen into the void.)* Yes… *(He folds up the board.)* On the other hand… *(He breaks the board over his knee.)* They are so much more reliable than friends… *(He slings it away.)*
GNASH:	You were born by a roadside, Kisster…
KISSTER:	It is the explanation for everything…
GNASH:	Your mother hid you in a drain…
KISSTER:	The drain was a friend…! *(He grins.)* It's true, but friendship wears you out. I am already fatigued at the prospect of satisfying you, who may have designs on my friendship for all I know…
GNASH:	I've none at all –
KISSTER:	I'm relieved to hear it. Help me kidnap an obnoxious girl.
GNASH:	You seen – kidnap…! Why kidnap? Why not play with her? Buy her an ice-cream?
KISSTER:	I am perfectly happy to buy her an ice-cream.
GNASH:	Charm, Kisster…!
KISSTER:	What do you know about charm? You are a spectacle of decrepitude.
GNASH:	Not always I wasn't, Kisster…
KISSTER:	Not always, that's what they all say, the old fool who could not tolerate being beaten at chess assures me he was a handsome ballroom champion who seduced the entire philosophy class at evening school. I believe him. But look at him now. No, charm is costly, let's kidnap her, and whatever charm I have she can discover later…
GNASH:	No.
KISSTER:	Yes.

GNASH:	No…!
KISSTER:	So much for friendship…!
GNASH:	Kisster –
KISSTER:	You come here –
GNASH:	Kisster –
KISSTER:	You drag you degenerating and –
GNASH:	Kisster –
KISSTER:	Malodorous remnant of female anatomy –
GNASH:	I'M NOT MALODOROUS…!
KISSTER:	Ranting and gesticulating –
GNASH:	I never ranted…!
KISSTER:	About the imperishable virtues of friendship and when I humbly propose a venture which puts it to the test –
GNASH:	I won't kidnap a girl.
	(Pause…KISSTER stretches…rubs his eyes.)
KISSTER:	Why not…? You were kidnapped yourself.
GNASH:	I was. I was and that is why I would never stoop to injure some poor –
KISSTER:	She isn't poor, she is inordinately rich.
GNASH:	All the same, I –
KISSTER:	Mrs Gnash, I know your history.
GNASH:	And I know yours…! You were born by a roadside. Planes swooped overhead –
KISSTER:	Quite so, and just as I recovered from these inauspicious beginnings, so you, as a consequence of being seized, became the mistress of a Syrian general –
GNASH:	Hideous –
KISSTER:	So you say –
GNASH:	Hideous ordeal –
KISSTER:	And subsequently a concubine in Tangier –
GNASH:	Worse, worse if anything –
KISSTER:	A Croatian brothel-keeper –
GNASH:	Who told you this…?
KISSTER:	It's from your own mouth, Mrs Gnash –
GNASH:	Never –
KISSTER:	And concluded your active years –

GNASH: Never –

KISSTER: As the mistress of a juvenile pick-pocket in
            Alsace-Lorraine –

GNASH: Not Alsace-Lorraine…!

KISSTER: Some frontier district, Mrs Gnash –

GNASH: Not Alsace-Lorraine…

KISSTER: A vivid and extraordinary career, which had you
            not been subjected to the privilege of kidnap,
            you could never have known…
            (Pause…she shrugs.)

GNASH: Look at me now…

KISSTER: Yes, but –

GNASH: Unadorned…

KISSTER: Yes, but –

GNASH: Unrequired…

KISSTER: Indeed –

GNASH: Uneverything…
            (Pause…she sits in a heap.)
            All right, Kisster…
            (She turns to him.)
            We will kidnap the rich girl who plays in the
            forest.

KISSTER: Oh, Mrs Gnash, I knew you would not
            disappoint me…! Your poverty and ugliness will
            be the perfect bait for any lurking sympathy that
            may exist in her arid and imperious soul…!

GNASH: Employ me, Kisster…!

KISSTER: I promise –

GNASH: *(Warming to the task.)* Use my expertise…!

KISSTER: It's vital, Mrs Gnash –

GNASH: My melancholy history – wring it, rinse it, put it
            through the mangle of your ambition, Kisster…

KISSTER: Yes, I will…

GNASH: Stitch the rotting rags of my old anguish into a
            hood with which to smother her…

KISSTER: I will…

GNASH: Block out the light and carry her away…

KISSTER: Yes…

What you describe…
Is precisely what I have in mind…
(COLOGNE enters, observing them.)

COLOGNE: Why do you sit with these unpleasant and undistinguished people when your cleverness entitles you to dine with eminent professors, Kisster? Great surgeons, opera singers, and the like? Our table is thick with invitations, not one of which is ever satisfied. Soon they will cease to invite us and all my efforts to announce your originality to the world will be rendered fatuous and absurd.

KISSTER: Yes. And not only are they undistinguished, in some instances they are utterly depraved.

COLOGNE: I'm certain of it.
(She extends a hand.)
Come home, now…

KISSTER: They also stink.

COLOGNE: Yes.

KISSTER: Stink and blaspheme.

COLOGNE: Yes.

KISSTER: *(Taking her hand.)* I hold them in the utmost contempt, and it occurs to me sometimes to drown them in a leaky barge…

COLOGNE: Is that so…? I don't think one needs to allow even a justifiable contempt to topple over into cruelty…

KISSTER: No…? Your hand is warm…!

COLOGNE: Is it…?

KISSTER: Warm, yes, and your hand is never warm…

COLOGNE: Never, it's true. Perhaps I was leaning on a radiator. I have just come from the library.

KISSTER: From the library…! And yet there is grass on your shoes…!

COLOGNE: *(Looking down.)* So there is…! I came across the lawns to be here…

KISSTER: And are there pine trees on the lawns?

COLOGNE: One or two perhaps…

KISSTER: Adorable Cologne…!
            (He looks to GNASH.)
            This is my tutor and my love…who lies to me
            to spare me pain whilst knowing in her heart I
            can't be lied to…
            (He bites his lip.)
            Adorable Cologne…
            Pity her…
            I've seen her naked under the moon…
COLOGNE: Shh…
GNASH: And me… He's seen me naked, too…!
KISSTER: Yes, but never under a moon…!
            *(He laughs, but the laugh slowly turns into a howl of
            despair. His shoulders quake. Sobs cascade from his
            tormented face, buried in COLOGNE's clothing.)*
MARSTON: *(Entering.)* Be a leader, little boy…
            *(They look at MARSTON. KISSTER ceases sobbing,
            wipes his eyes.)*
COLOGNE: He has every intention of distinguishing himself,
            thank you.
MARTSON: Be quiet, your hour's over…
COLOGNE: How dare you, I am the child's tutor.
MARSTON: The gong is sounding for you. Row silently.
            Tie the rowboat to the jetty and disappear, you
            Sunday loiterer…
COLOGNE: You are mad and impertinent. Kisster –
MARSTON: CAREFUL
            CAREFUL
            I HAVE MET MY DESTINY HERE
            *(He tosses a book to the ground… they look at it, not
            moving.)*
            It's all in the book.
            (Pause… they are apprehensive.)
COLOGNE: What is…? What is in the book…?
            (Pause. KISSTER goes to pick up the book.)
            Kisster…! Kisster…!
            (He stops in mid-reach.)
            Don't touch the book…

	(KISSTER remains half-stooping.)
GNASH:	Don't, Kisster…
COLOGNE:	Ignore the book. I will buy you an ice-cream in the palace gardens…
KISSTER:	Mint…?
COLOGNE:	Yes, mint…
GNASH:	Oh, I've seen those ices in the palace gardens…
KISSTER:	Really? How did you gain entrance to the palace gardens, I ask myself –
GNASH:	Mint…! Oh, mint…!
MARSTON:	*(To KISSTER.)* Ignore me and I will hang myself. *(Pause… KISSTER rises.)*
KISSTER:	What is it to me if you hang yourself? *(MARSTON shrugs.)* Given that I have not read the book, how can you deduce that I should mourn the death of its author? *(MARSTON shrugs again.)* Besides, if you hang yourself, you will never know that I might not, sitting in the palace gardens with a mint ice-cream, be overcome with regret, fling the spoon to the floor and pelt back here to retrieve your rather dirty little manifesto, a manifesto which you no doubt presume will change my life and subsequently, the lives of millions when I attain the supreme authority the manifesto is presumably designed to deliver into my hands. *(Uneasy laughter from all.)*
MARSTON:	I won't hang myself…
KISSTER:	No, do, do hang yourself, I was not dissuading you… *(MARSTON wipes his hands on his trousers, and picks the book off the floor. He dusts it.)*
MARSTON:	Often I have thought, there…there is the one…! And just as often I have seen the one prefer to eat ice-cream. *(He stuffs the book back in his pocket.)*

A life of injury. A career of bruise.

KISSTER: No less than you deserve, for failing to recognize that I, who was born at a roadside and nurtured in a drain, could not possibly be expected to immerse himself in a book which – by its very appearance – had obviously been offered time and time again to others, what do you take me for, the last resort?

(COLOGNE claps her hands with delight...MARSTON hangs his head.)

MARSTON: Pity...
Pity...
For obviously you are the one...

KISSTER: I am, I am the one...

MARTSON: Born by a roadside...reared in a drain...and yet –

KISSTER: A prodigy...! What more could you have asked for? Check all the drains, lift all the lids, who knows what other genius they conceal...

MARSTON: The perfect's unrepeatable...

KISSTER: Is that so...? But I must have the ice-cream that your appearance earned for me. Come, come, Cologne, to the palace gardens YOU WERE IN THE WOODS YOU SMELL OF IT she does there is a freshness in her clothes and her lips are sore from kissing as for your dog-eared book –

(He turns back to MARSTON.)

Let us be frank... all it contains you could whisper to me in a sentence...

MARSTON: On the contrary, it is itself the summary of twenty volumes...

(KISSTER smiles. He tugs at COLOGNE's hand.)

KISSTER: Take me away...! His eyes are odd...!

(They start to go out. Swiftly, MARSTON grabs GNASH and puts a knife to her throat. She lets out a single shriek. KISSTER and COLOGNE turn, amazed.)

MARTSON: Read it. Read my testament.

(Pause...KISSTER looks at the maddened figure of MARSTON.)

GNASH: Read it…
Read it, Kisster…
(Pause.)

KISSTER: I have a use for Mrs Gnash…
(He releases COLOGNE's hand and goes to MARSTON.)
Which must not be frustrated…
(He extends his hand to MARSTON. MARSTON holds out the book with his free hand. KISSTER takes it and swiftly leaves. COLOGNE hangs back.)

COLOGNE: He will not read it. Maniac. He will not read it.
(She follows KISSTER out… MARSTON keeps hold of GNASH.)

MARSTON: She says he will not read it…

GNASH: *(Terrified.)* He will…! I'm sure he will…!

MARSTON: But in any case, a perhaps with him is worth the certainty with fifty others…

GNASH: Oh, yes…!

MARSTON: For a great book is written for one pair of eyes, and one only…

GNASH: That's true…!

MARSTON: Is it? Is it true? What do you know?

GNASH: Nothing…

MARSTON: No, you know nothing, and you stink…
(He frees her with a violent thrust of his hand and goes out. GNASH sinks to the ground. GABRIELE enters…she observes the stricken woman…)

VII

GABRIELE: These woods are private.

GNASH: I know. I fell.

GABRIELE: You fell on private property.

GNASH: I apologize. Perhaps if you would help me up I could fall down again somewhere else.

GABRIELE: You are lucky I discovered you before the dogs. Given your powerful odours, I am surprised you were not tracked down and torn to pieces.

GNASH: I offended them also. Give us a hand, dear…

GABRIELE: I am not charitable, old hag…

GNASH: Nor was I…! So perhaps I'm not entitled to it. But extend a stick or something. I don't ask to touch your flesh…

GABRIELE: You are a hypocritical old bitch and I will whistle the dogs –

GNASH: Don't whistle…!
(Pause. She seeks to meet GABRIELE's eyes.)
If you knew love, you would not be cruel, I'm certain of it…

GABRIELE: I do know love. And I can see you have a hood concealed about you in which you and your accomplice plan to smother me.

GNASH: Accomplice…?
(GABRIELE whistles, clearly, shrilly.)
Oh…
(GNASH collapses in despair.)
Oh…
(KISSTER emerges from cover.)

KISSTER: You whistled me…?
(In alarm, GABRIELE whistles again, shrill and clear. No barking greets her appeal.)
I am the solitary hound today…

GNASH: Grab her, Kisster…

GABRIELE: Oh, you loathsome boy, you have poisoned my animals –

KISSTER: Yes, I could see no other way to persuade them.
(She turns to flee.)
Don't run…!
(She hesitates.)
Since you fell in love you aren't as swift as you were once. So much gratification subdues the limbs, whereas I, lean with hunger but unsatisfied, have all my energy to overtake you with…
(Pause.)

GABRIELE: My happiness enrages you.

KISSTER: Yes.

GNASH: Beat her…! Rope her, Kisster…! Pack her off to Syria…! They'll soon flatten her long nose…!

KISSTER: Shut up, you verminous detritus –

GNASH: Not so verminous you didn't disappear inside my clothes…! Not such detritus you could keep your paws out of –

KISSTER: I'll slit your throat –
            (GNASH is silent.)
            BEFORE MORE VILENESS BUBBLES OUT OF IT.
            (He looks to GABRIELE.) It's true, I've done things with her I shudder to acknowledge. But was I not born at a roadside? Was I not nurtured in a drain?

GABRIELE: And your misfortune entitles you to persecute a perfect stranger, does it?

KISSTER: Coercion comes in so many forms, of which pity is but one. Sometimes it arrives with hounds. Sometimes with hoods which hags fail to hide about their persons –

GNASH: Don't talk, bundle her up, Kisster…!

KISSTER: As for your being a perfect stranger, yes, you are perfect, but not a stranger to me, I've dreamed you and your nakedness will be familiar even as it is slowly unwrapped, there is a birthmark underneath your breast –

GABRIELE: Liar…!

GNASH: Bundle her, bundle her up…!

KISSTER: Your left breast, a pale print as if God Himself could not keep from touching you –

GABRIELE: *(In despair.)* Cologne has betrayed our intimacy…

KISSTER: Who can be trusted? Neither dogs nor locks on diaries keep me from my truth. My truth is you. Now, put her in the hood –

GABRIELE: Please, no hood…! I live my life outdoors,
            rooms suffocate me and I sleep on my father's
            roof even in blizzards…

KISSTER: You'll scream…

GABRIELE: I shan't –

KISSTER: You'll scream I've stolen you…

GABRIELE: I give my word –

GNASH: HER WORD WHAT'S THAT

GABRIELE: It's all I have.

GNASH: Kisster she's –
            (KISSTER silence GNASH with a withering glance.)

KISSTER: Say goodbye to your forests…
            (She closes her eyes.)
            I didn't hear…
            (She is still.)
            I must hear your adieus…

GABRIELE: *(Half-sobbing.)* Goodbye to my…
            *(KISSTER seizes her in his arms, smothering her with
            kisses and soothing her. The tears pour down his face.)*

GNASH: *(Apprehensive.)* Kisster…
            (The children wail.)
            Kisster…
            *(She looks around. She takes to her heels… KISSTER
            wipes his eyes… GABRIELE also.)*

KISSTER: My accomplice has deserted me…and with the
            hood…so…what I intended I… *(He shrugs.)*
            Perhaps another day…
            (He bites his lip.)

GABRIELE: Do you love me very much…?

KISSTER: *(His eyes downcast.)* I don't know…

GABRIELE: Do you think so much about me that you cannot
            sleep?

KISSTER: I don't know…

GABRIELE: You don't know…? You don't know if you sleep
            or not?

KISSTER: I sleep but –

GABRIELE: You sleep but my face appears to you? The
            movements of my hips disturb your rest?

KISSTER: I don't know what disturbs me but –

GABRIELE: My eyes, my limbs, my hair are –

KISSTER: IT'S TIME THESE FORESTS WERE BURNED DOWN.

    (Pause.)

    A match could do it, and a wind…sparks flying…branch to branch…deer fleeing… squirrels…voles… AND ON THE ASHES HUGE STADIUMS WHERE THE POPULATIONS OF THE CITIES SHOUT ONE WORD…

GABRIELE: What word?

    (KISSTER smiles.)

KISSTER: Gabriele…

    (She smiles…half-reluctant…a voice is heard.)

MENDEL: GAB-RIELE…

    (The smile disappears as a man enters. He examines KISSTER.)

    What's privacy but temptation? What's secrecy but violation? Answer, you're clever. And every fence, what is it but a thing to leap? Answer, you're clever. Shall I never find a place sufficiently obscure in which to conceal myself without inflaming envy and intrusion? Answer. I'll kill for peace. And yet that stimulates further invasion. Answer…!

    Answer…!

KISSTER: It's her…

    (Pause.)

    She…

    (Pause.)

    I…

    (Pause.)

    Don't beat me I was born at a roadside –

MENDEL: Me, too.

KISSTER: Is that so…!

MENDEL: Planes swooped low, the rattle of their cannon shook the air and flung great clods of earth

across my mother's body, I trace my love of
silence to those first hours, why is it her?

KISSTER: Some…
She…
(Pause…he shrugs.)
Her skin has this…
I'm drawn by her odour DON'T KILL ME
I'd scale a fence of bells just to come near her
DON'T STAB ME AND BURY ME IN A
HOLE she lives as if the world was empty
DON'T DON'T and smells like the first
woman must have smelled NO SINGLE BELL
WOULD I DISLODGE SO SCRUPULOUS
WOULD I BE CUNNING SUBTLE AND
METICULOUS PITY ME I am an orphan
probably I should go home now yes it's time a
man gave me a book and still I haven't read it
so… *(He falters.)*

MENDEL: Breathe her. Breathe my daughter, now.
(Pause.)

KISSTER: Breathe your –

MENDEL: INHALE HER…
She intoxicates you, does she not…?
INHALE HER, THEN…
*(GABRIELE laughs…she extends a hand towards
KISSTER, presenting the back. KISSTER goes to her,
sniffs her hand…his eyes rise to MENDEL's gaze.)*
Yes…?
*(KISSTER travels the length of her arm inhaling…
GABRIELE laughs… KISSTER looks at MENDEL.)*
Go on…
(Pause.)
Breathe…! Breathe…!
*(KISSTER pulls away her thin dress, revealing her
shoulder. He proceeds to inhale the odours of her neck.)*

GABRIELE: It tickles…!

MENDEL: BREATHE…

KISSTER: I am… I am breathing…

MENDEL:	BREATHE DEEPER THEN OF MY DAUGHTER…
KISSTER:	Yes…

(With a sudden movement, KISSTER tears the dress from GABRIELE down to her waist. She shudders. KISSTER hesitates, expecting a blow from MENDEL which does not arrive. KISSTER presses his face to GABRIELE's body. She is pale, drawn with anxiety. KISSTER breathes deeply.)

MENDEL:	BREATHE…!

(KISSTER inhales dizzily.)

NO, BREATHE…

(The odour has the effect of a narcotic. KISSTER begins to laugh, to hallucinate. He goes to drag the dress from the hips of the girl, and tugs at the cloth, which is stubborn. GABRIELE's frightened eyes remain on her father, who, as KISSTER becomes more infatuated, goes to him and drapes a silk handkerchief over his head. KISSTER is still. MENDEL extends a hand to GABRIELE. She takes it. They walk silently off. KISSTER remains kneeling in this position for a long time. TUESDAY appears…he steps nearer, examining KISSTER with a certain apprehension. Suddenly, KISSTER tears the silk from his head.)

KISSTER:	Why do they lie? Why? Why all this lying?
TUESDAY:	You lie yourself…!
KISSTER:	Only because I'm weak…!

(He rises to his feet.)

When I am strong, then I'll cease lying…

TUESDAY:	My father wants to beat you, I must warn you…
KISSTER:	Everyone is out to beat me…
TUESDAY:	For trying to undress my mother…
KISSTER:	Perhaps I love your mother and therefore to undress her is my right.
TUESDAY:	YOU ARE VILE AND DON'T LOVE ANYONE…!
KISSTER:	How would you know?

TUESDAY:	YOU DON'T, YOU DON'T LOVE ANYONE...
KISSTER:	No, no, I don't, but frequently I think I do, Tuesday, I poisoned seven hounds for love, they writhed and stared at me with such appealing eyes, but I was pitiless, for dogs are liars also, if I had not exterminated them what would they not have done to me? I did not think however, of poisoning their master...
TUESDAY:	You should poison yourself...!
KISSTER:	Perhaps I will, perhaps someone who is so frequently betrayed as me should pay the world a brief visit and in disgust, turn his face to the wall...
TUESDAY:	Don't, Kisster, please...
KISSTER:	It is air she smells of. But air so pure, one does not immediately recognize the smell as air at all...
TUESDAY:	Leave my mother alone, Kisster...
KISSTER:	Your mother...?
	(He looks at TUESDAY thoughtfully.)
	The more you plead, the more anxious I become to have her naked in a bed with me –
TUESDAY:	YOU DISGUST ME YOU DISGUST ME YOU –
KISSTER:	Yes yes yes
	I KNOW I DO
	But I was not talking of your mother, who smells not so much of air as kitchens...
	(Pause.)
	Which is a decent smell...which is not a bad thing to smell of, after all...
	(Pause...TUESDAY stares, his brows knitted.)
TUESDAY:	Why do I like you...?
KISSTER:	I suppose because... I like myself...
	(He takes TUESDAY roughly by the arm.)

I require things of the world which possibly
the world can never give me…which the world
perhaps…does not possess…
(TUESDAY looks at his friend.)

TUESDAY: I'll try… I'll see if I can… I'll ask my mother to
undress if that's –

KISSTER: Yes, do ask her…
(He smiles.)
The world I think is everything…but poor…
Oh, Tuesday, how poor the world's everything
is…!

TUESDAY: *(Shrugging his shoulders.)* I don't know, Kisster, I
have not seen everything yet –

KISSTER: What have you not seen yet, Tuesday?

TUESDAY: What have I –

KISSTER: Yes, what have you not seen yet?
(TUESDAY flusters.)
The Taj Mahal…? The pyramids…?

TUESDAY: Of course I haven't seen the pyramids –

KISSTER: The Great Wall of China –

TUESDAY: No, I haven't seen that yet –

KISSTER: It's in your mother's cunt, Tuesday…
(TUESDAY reels…falters…his eyes close…)

TUESDAY: I should kill you… I should find a branch and
beat you round the head…

KISSTER: Yes…

TUESDAY: I should beat you till the brains came out…
(They spontaneously clasp one another.)
Kisster…you are mad…

KISSTER: Oh, yes, mad because I have ceased to admire
the world…mad, obviously…
*(A figure enters. The figure stares, and drops to the
ground.)*

VIII

TUESDAY:	That –
KISSTER:	Certainly –
TUESDAY:	That –
KISSTER:	Positively –
TUESDAY:	That –
KISSTER:	*(Swiftly drawing out of his pocket the silk handkerchief given him by MENDEL.)* Breathe through this…! *(They smother their mouths and noses. They stare at the inert form…it lifts an arm. The arm falls.*
TUESDAY:	PLAGUE…! *(TUESDAY goes to take flight but KISSTER catches his arm and swings him about.)*
KISSTER:	If I do not love the world…and yet the world, having no values, does not care whether I love it or not…my death from plague should be neither feared by me nor regarded with apprehension by the world… *(He goes nearer, his hand still held by TUESDAY, who is motionless.)* Such a condition of perfect indifference on both sides is possibly the best protection – *(He goes nearer.)* from the disease – *(He touches the body with a finger and withdraws it again.)* TUESDAY…! *(He is half-hysterical. He swings about. He peers over TUESDAY's shoulder at the inert form.)* Your turn…
TUESDAY:	What…?
KISSTER:	Your turn…
TUESDAY:	My turn…but I like the world…
KISSTER:	Precisely, and because you like it, Tuesday, you have an obligation to encounter it –
TUESDAY:	Do I –

KISSTER: In every form…
(Pause. TUESDAY, holding KISSTER's hand in his left, reaches to the body with his right, the finger-tips extended. Suddenly the body springs into activity, clasping TUESDAY in its arms and dragging him into a rolling embrace, smothering his face with kisses. KISSTER watches with horror. TUESDAY screams, the body laughs, frees TUESDAY and lies on its back, weak from its exertions… TUESDAY scrambles up, spitting and wiping his mouth with his hands, pale-faced and devastated by horror…he stops, staring at KISSTER.)

TUESDAY: MO–THER…!

KISSTER: I'll tell her – I'll – no, I can't, your father might be –

TUESDAY: OH, MO–THER…!

KISSTER: All right, all right –
(TUESDAY starts to run off.)
TUESDAY, DO NOT RUN…
(TUESDAY stops, turns, tears pouring down his cheeks.)
Don't run because…you must not run…
(TUESDAY lifts a helpless hand…)
Or touch people, you –

TUESDAY: Liar…

KISSTER: Me…?

TUESDAY: Liar, yes…death horrifies you…you are desperate to live…!
(Injured by the rebuke, KISSTER lifts both his hands to take TUESDAY's, but TUESDAY declines them and hurries off, calling his mother…in the silence, the body speaks…)

RAGSIT: You next…
(He laughs…KISSTER turns to him.)

KISSTER: Me next? How? I haven't seen the Taj Mahal.
(He goes nearer to RAGSIT.)
Kiss me, now…
Smother me…
Infect…
Infect…!

> *(He kneels beside RAGSIT, who is suspicious, and stares. Suddenly he spits once into KISSTER's face. KISSTER coolly wipes the sputum away with his hand. RAGSIT spits again… KISSTER wipes this away… they exchange long looks, then RAGSIT seizes KISSTER by the hand.)*

RAGSIT: Oh, my life's a shame…! A shame…!

KISSTER: To whom…?

RAGSIT: To me…!

KISSTER: Yes…

> *(RAGSIT weeps.)*

Yes…

It's ugly, your life, certainly…

> *(He goes to get up.)*

RAGSIT: Don't go…!

> *(He looks piteously at KISSTER.)*

Stay with me…

Until I'm gone…

Please stay with me…

KISSTER: Until you're gone? That could be hours…!

> *(He remembers something. He feels for his back pocket.)*

Still –

> *(He pulls out the dog-eared pamphlet.)*

I have a book…!

RAGSIT: Read the book…!

KISSTER: Read it, yes…! I'll read the book because anything you have to say is probably less interesting than what is in the book, and anyway in your condition, even if it were not in the least interesting, you are unlikely to complain, all you require is the familiar sound of human speech, I have no doubt you would be satisfied to hear me read a shopping list, which this may be, for all I know, I have yet to read it – oh, it is a shopping list…!

> *(He looks at RAGSIT.)*

RAGSIT: Read…

Read…!

KISSTER: A shopping list of propositions…!

RAGSIT: Read…!

KISSTER: *(Reading.)* To Him For Whom The World Is
Shit…
(He reflects.)
That's only the dedication..!
(He looks at RAGSIT.)

RAGSIT: Read…!

KISSTER: I am reading, but sometimes I must comment on
what I am reading –

RAGSIT: Comment…!

KISSTER: One must engage with works of literature, one
must invest one's energies in them or –

RAGSIT: Invest…!

KISSTER: Thank you, I will. My ancient tutor, when he
was not struggling to urinate on me or force me
to urinate on him, impressed upon me the vital
necessity to be engaged by works of art –

RAGSIT: Engage, then…!

KISSTER: *(Returning to the text.)* Page 2…
(He folds back the cover, in an earnest fashion…)
The pages are falling out…it's obvious this
particular edition has been through many
hands…

RAGSIT: It's true…!

KISSTER: What is?

RAGSIT: What he says –

KISSTER: Where?

RAGSIT: In the – in the – what is it?

KISSTER: The dedication –

RAGSIT: The dedication, yes –

KISSTER: On the world being shit?

RAGSIT: It is shit –

KISSTER: Yes – this is the book for you – page 2 –

RAGSIT: Shit –

KISSTER: *(Reading.)* 'To be born is to be abused…'

RAGSIT: Yes…! Yes…!

KISSTER: You concur with this also?

RAGSIT: Concur, yes…!

KISSTER: I'll read on –
           (He stops, however, catching a glimpse of a movement nearby.)
RAGSIT: Read...! Comment...! Engage...!
           (KISSTER is staring at COLOGNE, who has appeared and stands anxiously, as if at a rendezvous...she appears unaware of KISSTER or RAGSIT. KISSTER returns to the book.)
KISSTER: *(Reading.)* 'The horror of birth is merely the first instalment of that deluge of pain which is our only common destiny...'
RAGSIT: True...! True...! Who was this man...?
KISSTER: 'Forgetfulness alone permits continuation of a life, which memory would condemn as unsupportable –'
RAGSIT: Oh, yes...! Oh, yes, again...!
KISSTER: 'And every passing pleasure only serves to –'
           (He stops, seeing GABRIELE rush into COLOGNE's arms. They embrace passionately... Pause.)
RAGSIT: Serves to what...?
           (KISSTER is transfixed by the spectacle.)
           To what...! *(Pause.)*
           TO WHAT DOES IT SERVE...!
           TO WHAT...!
           TO WHAT...!
           (KISSTER rises to his feet, the book hangs limply in his hand...the embrace of the two women lingers, a picture of profound intimacy...at last KISSTER turns back to RAGSIT, who is dead.)
KISSTER: To smother solitude... I expect...
           (The women part, their hands locked together... they are reluctant to let go...at last GABRIELE tears free and runs off. COLOGNE, turning, is surprised to encounter KISSTER.)
           I was born at a roadside...
COLOGNE: Yes, so you were...
KISSTER: So many things I want and...! Oh, so many I can't have...
COLOGNE: Yes...

KISSTER: So many things for which being born at a
roadside has simply not entitled me…
(COLOGNE shrugs.)
Would I not have been better born in a bed…?
Not any bed, Cologne, but an almighty bed, a
monarch of beds surmounted by the eagle crest
of my own dynasty?
(She shrugs again.)

COLOGNE: Perhaps…

KISSTER: It's possible I have the plague…
(She flinches. He laughs.)
You see…!
THE HORROR GRIPS YOU AND IT WAS
ME YOU LOVED…!
(He smiles, wanly.)
Oh, how you dread some sickness that will part
you from your ecstasy…

COLOGNE: Yes…of course… *(She is on guard.)*

KISSTER: Don't be afraid… I shan't smother you with my
contagion…even if…I feel perfectly entitled to…
(COLOGNE closes her eyes.)

COLOGNE: You are such a clever –

KISSTER: Such a clever –

COLOGNE: Such a clever –

KISSTER: Clever –

COLOGNE: Boy…
(They laugh.)

KISSTER: And yet…
How inefficacious this cleverness is…
(He suddenly clasps his head…)
Fever…! *(His eyes glow with alarm.)*

COLOGNE: Kisster…!

KISSTER: Stay back…! You have a love to live for…!

COLOGNE: Kisster – *(She moves towards him.)*

KISSTER: Stay…!
STAY…!
(COLOGNE stops in her movement…he smiles.)
You are…
(He shakes his head.)

You are able to stay…
(She stares…he is seized by a resolution.)
I'll lie here…it's better all the victims should
arrange themselves in piles…for ease of burial
and so on…

COLOGNE: Kisster…

KISSTER: Tuesday also, he is ill, and the world without
Tuesday is impossible to contemplate for me, so –

COLOGNE: Kisster…

KISSTER: Shh…don't grieve…
(He arranges himself on the ground.)
This is…as comfortable as the sick deserve…
and those who were born at roadsides have a
positive nostalgia for –
(She laughs.)
Yes…for damp and sordid places, which this is not,
this wood has much to recommend it, indeed, if I
were not mortally ill, but merely enjoying the idea
of being mortally ill, I should certainly say, what
better place to perish than this wood –
(She laughs again.)
How you will miss me, Cologne, no cleverer
person will cross your path…

COLOGNE: No…

KISSTER: And the plans you had for me…! Oh, the
plans…!
(He crosses his hands on his chest.)
Nothing less than the governance of the world…
(She goes to rush to him.)
No…! *(She stops.)*
Walk backwards, I insist…withdraw…until our
eyes…for all their passionate ecstasy…can't find
the subject of their longing any more…
*(COLOGNE obeys, withdrawing step by step…
KISSTER stares…and stares…his head writhes…then
sinks…at last his hand gropes about for the book once
more…he is about to open it when he becomes aware
of a stranger observing him.)*

IX

SCHOCK: Scum.

KISSTER: Yes, but dying…

SCHOCK: My son adored you and you are scum. *(Pause.)*

KISSTER: We…

The pair of us…

Mutually concluded…

Life did not justify the effort necessary to endure it…

SCHOCK: Scum…

KISSTER: Yes, a parent would adopt that attitude, but –

SCHOCK: I LOVED MY BOY AND YOU STOLE HIM FROM ME.

(Pause.)

KISSTER: Certainly I exercised an influence on Tuesday, but his affection for you never faltered, and –

(A woman enters…she stands a little distance away, also observing.)

My fever is subsiding…evidently, I am immune…

SCHOCK: Never from my vengeance – *(He catches sight of his wife.)*

DON'T WATCH –

(SCHOCK snatches up a fallen branch. KISSTER swiftly adopts the posture of a penitent.)

KISSTER: Behold a boy executed in a forest, his body left for foxes and for wolves, whose only crime was –

SCHOCK: *(As his wife comes nearer.)* DON'T WATCH –

KISSTER: If this is crime – to have –

SCHOCK: DON'T WATCH I SAID –

KISSTER: Disagreed with God…

(SCHOCK hangs suspended between will and the performance.)

TERESA: Strike…

(SCHOCK wavers.)

Strike, then…

(And wavers more.)
Or don't…
(He still wavers, agonized.)
Oh, do or don't…!
(He throws down the branch in frustration. He smothers his head in his hands. TERESA watches his grief with a dispassionate expression… Then goes to KISSTER, and draws his head to her apron.)

KISSTER: You smell of bread…
(He lifts her skirt. He explores her beneath. TERESA does nothing to impede him. SCHOCK, aware of this activity, does nothing either, but stares resolutely into the distance. TERESA catches her breath, gasps. Her head falls back. She gasps again. She is still. SCHOCK turns round. A certain purposefulness affects him.)

SCHOCK: These bodies…left to decay…will only breed further diseases…

KISSTER: Yes…the able-bodied certainly should congregate with shovels, excavate deep pits, and try to keep pace with the ravages of the plague…

SCHOCK: Obviously, yes – *(He seems to be about to set off.)*

KISSTER: Others, to offset the decimation of the population –
(SCHOCK stops in mid-movement.)
Should fornicate with fertile women –

SCHOCK: Yes –

KISSTER: Rather as wasps, without dissension, divide themselves into those who work and those who love, both forms of labour equally essential to the continued prosperity of the colony…

SCHOCK: Yes…
(Pause.)

KISSTER: Hurry then…!
(SCHOCK looks, hesitates, then hurtles off…pause.)

TERESA: You are such a – such a – such a clever child…
(Pause. KISSTER examines TERESA.)

KISSTER: How like my beloved Tuesday his father is…it is as if…knowing the place of his conception…the odour of the womb…he lives…!

TERESA: WHEN WERE YOU A CHILD WHENEVER WERE YOU KISSTER WHEN A CHILD…!
            (KISSTER shrugs at her sudden vehemence.)

KISSTER: I don't know…

TERESA: NEVER A CHILD…

KISSTER: No, and never to be adult either…
            (TERESA kisses him spontaneously on the mouth…she withdraws, pensively.)
            I have no mother…!
            (TERESA stops.)
            And my governess…my teacher…has betrayed me for a shallow girl…

TERESA: What could I teach you, Kisster…?
            (He looks blankly at her.)
            And what kind of mother would I be…seeing that to take you in my bed is all my ambition…?

KISSTER: I couldn't say…but if we have a child, your husband must father it, because he's good and will protect it, whereas my mind's inconstant, I should put it down and forget where I had left it –

TERESA: Far better he –

KISSTER: Far better, yes…
            (She laughs…him also…he runs to her.)
            Oh, Tuesday's mother…! Do not die…!
            (They swiftly hold hands. TERESA departs…shovels are flung on stage. A cacophony of clattering iron. A man enters, elegant, correct. He sits on a chair.)

X

OLMUTZ:	And have you finished this peculiar not to say morbid not to say unhealthy intimacy with the destitute and the diseased their company not to speak of their odour must have become familiar to the point of nausea I daresay have you finished we ask ourselves have you or is it merely hesitation possibly a gasp for air before further immersion so many like the poor but always for dishonest reasons –
KISSTER:	Finished and so finished I cannot even by the most strenuous efforts recall their fascination –
OLMUTZ:	I speak brutally –
KISSTER:	I prefer it –
OLMUTZ:	Brutally because you spot a lie more swiftly than a heron falls on its prey –
KISSTER:	Faster than a heron, yes –
OLMUTZ:	And we are so glad so glad you have emerged we waited oh how we waited for your emergence –
KISSTER:	It takes time –
OLMUTZ:	To emerge takes time and we were patient –
KISSTER:	You were patient, I was young –
OLMUTZ:	Young yes and yet with you the very concepts of maturity and immaturity seem strangely inapposite –
KISSTER:	I was born by a roadside –
OLMUTZ:	By a roadside, yes, and this cannot be sufficiently stressed perhaps –
KISSTER:	Never sufficiently stressed –
OLMUTZ:	By those who wish to reach some understanding of your extraordinary –
KISSTER:	My mother hid me in a drain –
OLMUTZ:	This drain might be alone responsible for –
KISSTER:	Oh, yes –
OLMUTZ:	You think the drain? You identify the drain specifically as a component of your –

KISSTER: Yes, oh, yes –

OLMUTZ: Kisster, we are so very oh so very gratified some doubted never me however some said he cannot possibly emerge the crime the violence the addiction never me however –

KISSTER: The drain assisted me –

OLMUTZ: The drain again –

KISSTER: By being simultaneously a preparation for and a deterrent to all squalor and infection –

OLMUTZ: Yes –

(A second man enters.)

This is Kisster…!

(KISSTER turns to see PRESSBURG…a pause.)

PRESSBURG: Kisster, who else…? Have we not studied you…?

(They exchange a long stare.)

Through telescopes…

KISSTER: I felt the glare…

PRESSBURG: And interrogations of your intimates…

KISSTER: They warned me of your persistence saying old men were agitated pale old men in summer suits with skin like deer I was not unduly anxious what are you magistrates collectors anthropologists not unduly anxious and I have been urinated over beaten by a spiteful girl and kissed by dead men read this it has altered my life…

(He extends the little book to OLMUTZ and PRESSBURG. They make no effort to examine it…his hand remains extended.)

Perhaps you know it already…

(Pause. He does not withdraw the book.)

Perhaps your lives already are suffused in its teaching…as last season's fruits are bottled in strange alcohols…

(He still extends the book…they feel constrained… PRESSBURG takes it.)

PRESSBURG: Not a very nice book…

KISSTER: Not a nice book, no, and made of such poor paper…

PRESSBURG: As for the binding…

KISSTER: No binding at all…! It is held together only by the solidarity of its thoughts…
(It hangs from PRESSBURG's fingers.)

OLMUTZ: Thank God you emerged…!

KISSTER: Thank God I did –
(PRESSBURG tears the book across… KISSTER's mouth hangs open…the pages float to the floor…a long and menacing pause ensues.)

PRESSBURG: Everything changes…

OLMUTZ: And what was oh so very very
DEFINITIVE
in our natures what was
ESSENCE
in our perception of ourselves
is discovered after all to have been purely
PROVISIONAL…
(Pause… KISSTER's gaze lifts from the floor.)

KISSTER: I have a feeling that I was not invited here to piss in your mouths…
(Pause.)
Beat you at chess…
(Pause.)
Or infect you with the plague…
(Pause.)
Which is a pity because any one of those I might manage without undue –
PICK UP THE BOOK YOU GREY LOUT YOU DESECRATOR
(OLMUTZ and PRESSBURG laugh…in the following silence, KISSTER smiles.)
It's true that in years to come I might well find this text unappetizing…the ideas repetitive…
and the style uneducated…yes….possibly
your vandalism is only the acceleration of an inevitable but dilatory decay…

(All three laugh…)

OLMUTZ: Do not resist us, Kisster…

PRESSBURG: You are such a clever –

OLMUTZ: Such a –

PRESSBURG: Such a clever boy –

OLMUTZ: And this cleverness, this infinite cleverness,
             might enable you to hold out for decades –

PRESSBURG: First one tactic –

OLMUTZ: Then another –

PRESSBURG: One deception –

OLMUTZ: On another –

PRESSBURG: And we're not young…!
             (Pause.)

KISSTER: You want to help me…
             (Pause.)
             You want to help me –

PRESSBURG: Not you –

OLMUTZ: You, yes –

PRESSBURG: You, of course –

OLMUTZ: You but not only you –

PRESSBURG: Not you –

KISSTER: Not me –

PRESSBURG: Not you in the last resort –

OLMUTZ: Nor the first instance, either –

PRESSBURG: You and the world together –

KISSTER: The world –

PRESSBURG: The world of which you are a part –

OLMUTZ: But no more than a part –

PRESSBURG: You therefore but –

KISSTER: Not me at all…
             *(Pause… KISSTER laughs…their eyes are locked in
             interrogation.)*
             You are worried for the world… *(He bites his lip.)*
             Because I'm in it…
             AND I THOUGHT YOU LOVED ME…!
             I THOUGHT THESE OLD GREY MEN
             WITH SKIN LIKE DEER THEY WANT TO
             DRINK MY URINE…!

(Pause.)

I must grow up quicker…it has taken me all of five minutes to discover your intentions LOVE NO DID I SAY LOVE SOMETHING AKIN TO LOVE AND I'M NOT A SPECIALIST five minutes thank God I was born at a roadside had I not been oh five hours five days even it might have required to discern it murder me why don't you murder surely is the solution its brevity its efficacy murder in the public interest I am immune to plague but not to poison I daresay –

OLMUTZ: Kisster, tell us of one happiness –

KISSTER: One happiness –

OLMUTZ: One happiness, Kisster, that befell you –

KISSTER: One –

OLMUTZ: One will do…

    (Pause. KISSTER appears to reflect.)

KISSTER: One…

PRESSBURG: One…

    (Pause.)

KISSTER: One…

    (Pause.)

OLMUTZ: Perhaps there is not one…

KISSTER: It's – it's –

OLMUTZ: Perhaps, Kisster, you have yet to know one –

PRESSBURG: Oh, Kisster, there is not one –

KISSTER: Yes –

PRESSBURG: Is there…? Is there one…?

KISSTER: Yes – when Gabriele beat me with a stick…!

    (He grins.)

OLMUTZ: And was that happiness, Kisster…to be beaten with a stick…?

KISSTER: No, to be beaten with a stick is not happiness, but to be beaten with a stick by Gabriele…

    (Pause.)

PRESSBURG: Kisster –

OLMUTZ: Kisster –

KISSTER: I am not immune to poisons…did I say…?

(Pause. They stare at KISSTER.)

PRESSBURG: How you would like that…how you would
prefer it…

KISSTER: Would I…

PRESSBURG: Oh, yes, greatly prefer it, because then you
could say, look, I am not loved…!

OLMUTZ: As you writhed on the ground, indulge yourself
with the perverse reflection that you had
frustrated every gesture of kindness or warmth –

PRESSBURG: The grotesque confirmation of you own spiritual
deformity

OLMUTZ: Never –

PRESSBURG: Never, Kisster –

OLMUTZ: Ask for poison –

PRESSBURG: You are loved… *(Pause.)*

KISSTER: Loved… *(Pause.)*
By whom…?
(They are silent. KISSTER is filled with apprehension.)
By you… *(Pause.)*
I'm loved by you and you are angels…
(They do not contradict him.)
Angels, obviously…
(Pause.)
The love of angels is a funny love coming as
it must from will and not desire I have never
willed love either it announced itself or it did
not I don't think love of your kind recommends
itself to me –

PRESSBURG: It cannot be refused, Kisster –

KISSTER: All the same, I –

PRESSBURG: Still, it's there –

KISSTER: All right, it's there –

OLMUTZ: Irrefutable –

PRESSBURG: Inextinguishable –

KISSTER: What is it? A bandage round a dog? I've seen
dogs tear off bandages –

PRESSBURG: They bleed…!

KISSTER: Bleed, yes, the horror of the bandage…!

PRESSBURG: BUT IT HEALS…

OLMUTZ: IT HEALS…
(They appeal to him…he shifts…he turns one way in his chair…then another.)

KISSTER: It's false…
(They are patient.)
It's false…it's…
(He struggles.)
I'm only a boy, I can't –
(The angels are triumphant.)

OLMUTZ: Only a boy…!

PRESSBURG: But what a boy…!

OLMUTZ: Such a –

PRESSBURG: Such a –

OLM/PRESS: SUCH A CLEVER BOY…!
(They smile, kindly.)

PRESSBURG: I believe that is a sentence you have never framed before…

OLMUTZ: Kisster, you are indeed a boy…

PRESSBURG: Rejoice in your boyhood…
(He stares, squirms.)

KISSTER: No…!

PRESSBURG: Kisster –

OLMUTZ: LUXURIATE IN YOUR PERFECT INNOCENCE…
(He struggles.)

KISSTER: No…!
No because it's false –

PRESSBURG: What falsehood?

KISSTER: You are coercing me…you say you are loving me, but you are coercing me…yes…this love is not love but rather fear…you fear me, and think to stifle my character by –

OLMUTZ: It is not your character –

KISSTER: No? Not my character? What is my character, then?
(They smile.)

OLMUTZ: We see your character…but by bit…we see the
               character of Kisster as an object of great beauty,
               encrusted by the grime of unkindness and
               misuse. How it shines, Kisster…we the polish…
               you the brass…!
               (Pause.)
               Probably, for one day, that's enough…

PRESSBURG: Enough polishing for one day…

OLMUTZ: *(Smiling.)* Our arms ache…!
               (KISSTER does not move.)
               Come back tomorrow…!

PRESSBURG: Or the next day…

OLMUTZ: Or the next day, please yourself…!
               *(They stand, as if to usher him out. He remains fixedly
               in his chair.)*

KISSTER: Bring me Gabriele. *(Pause.)*

OLMUTZ: Gabriele? But she hits you with sticks…!
               (They laugh.)

PRESSBURG: Come back tomorrow…!

OLMUTZ: Or the next day, please yourself…!
               (He is recalcitrant.)

KISSTER: Gabriele then I will. *(Pause.)*

OLMUTZ: Will what, Kisster…?
               (He shrugs.)

KISSTER: Cease to be myself…
               (They smile…they shake their heads.)

OLMUTZ: And did we say that Kisster should cease to be
               himself?

PRESSBURG: The opposite.

OLMUTZ: Kisster will come to Kisster, and throwing his
               arms round him, will say, I fled you, and you are
               beautiful…
               (Pause.)

KISSTER: *(Doggedly.)* Gabriele…

PRESSBURG: Of course Gabriele…! What kept her from you?
               Only yourself…!

OLMUTZ: Come back tomorrow…!

PRESSBURG: Or the next day…!

OLMUTZ: Gabriele, obviously…!
          (They go out. KISSTER remains seated…he smiles.)
KISSTER: I bribed the angels…! *(He bites his lip.)*
          Or did they bribe me…?
          (He jumps off the chair as a covered hospital trolley drifts in and stops.)

XI

KISSTER: Certainly a consequence of being born by a roadside must be this…
          (He advances towards the trolley, cautiously.)
          That the general insecurity of things…
          (He puts a hand to the cloth.)
          The prevailing unpredictability…
          (He lifts the corner but looks away.)
          Equips me for –
          (He drops it again. He goes to the other side.)
          All manner of surprises –
          (He lifts that edge.)
          Never do I say –
          As some would say –
          (He looks away resolutely.)
          I PROTEST AT THIS I RAGE I
          On the contrary I possess the uncritical demeanour of an animal a bird for whom all alteration is –
          (He looks at the hand revealed.)
          No more nor less to be repudiated than…
          (He lets the cloth fall.)
          The hour of the sunrise…
          COL–OGNE…!
          COL–OGNE…!
          OH, MY DEAR MY DEAR MY DEAR COLOGNE…!
          (He wails, sobs, staggers, then turning he pulls away the sheet that covers her in a single movement…he

177

holds it limply, staring at COLOGNE's body, which
lies in a simple shift.)
Perhaps all those who betray me die…
All those who fail to measure up to my…
AND SUCH LITTLE FEET
SUCH MISSHAPEN LITTLE FEET –
This explanation surely for her extravagance her
prodigality in little boots or did the little boots
contribute to the feet the ugliness the cramped
and crushed appearance of the feet
WHAT PROFOUNDLY AND
OFFENSIVELY UNLOVELY FEET I
COULD ALMOST I COULD CUT OFF THE
FEET
(He smothers the feet of the body with the sheet. He
becomes aware of the gaze of a mortician.)
Plague, was it…?

CANNAY: Suicide.
                (Pause. KISSTER tears off the sheet again.)

KISSTER: These feet, have you observed them? In all
                your years have you observed such spoiled and
                sordid feet?

CANNAY: I don't make a point of –

KISSTER: Come here and tell me –

CANNAY: Feet are feet –

KISSTER: If you have ever witnessed such
                (Pause.)
                Why suicide
                What's your evidence
                I have it on authority some plague victims show
                signs of toxic poisoning
                The toes are mashed together I wonder how she
                walked and yet she did she walked with perfect
                what a walk she had all men admired it
                Do look
                It's a case of plague and you have –

CANNAY: The wrists, silly.
                (Pause.)

KISSTER: Don't call me silly.
(Pause.)
I am a boy but –

CANNAY: I'm sorry –

KISSTER: Not all boys are silly and –
(He looks at the narrow bandages on COLOGNE's wrists.)
Yes
She
Thank you for bandaging her wrists and where's the letter she was painfully literate and never
I DO THINK THE FEET COULD BE REMOVED DON'T YOU
(Pause. CANNAY comes to the end of the trolley.)
HACKED
HACKED OFF…?
(CANNAY looks at KISSTER.)

CANNAY: You must forgive… *(Pause.)*

KISSTER: I do, I forgive everything but these feet…
(Pause.)

CANNAY: Please yourself –

KISSTER: I WAS BORN BY A ROADSIDE
And your exhortations are worthless, pitiful and absurd as the defunct currency of an overthrown regime…
(CANNAY shrugs.)

CANNAY: Grief…
Its teeth…
(He wanders out. In a sudden spasm of bitterness and love, KISSTER smothers the feet of the body with kisses.)

KISSTER: Cologne.
Oh, Cologne.
There are three forms of coercion…

GABRIELE: *(Entering.)* And the greatest of these…
(KISSTER looks up from the body. GABRIELE is looking at him, coolly.)
What is the greatest, Kisster…?

(He chooses not to reply.)
I look at her
I look down on Cologne
And I say I am not moved to pity
I am not persuaded by her argument
Nor am I ashamed
(Pause…she lifts the hem of the sheet.)
She perished…
And I was not coerced…
(She covers COLOGNE with a sweep of her arm.)

KISSTER: I smell your body…
GABRIELE: Yes…
KISSTER: The fourth coercion, surely…?
GABRIELE: Yes…! *(She turns swiftly to him.)*
I have a man, Kisster.
KISSTER: A man…
GABRIELE: And he will possibly destroy my life…
KISSTER: He destroyed Cologne's, evidently… *(Pause.)*
I have however, the promise of the angels that whatever –
GABRIELE: Angels –
KISSTER: Fatuous obsession pulps and spoils your soul –
GABRIELE: Angels…!
KISSTER: Angels yes…!
GABRIELE: Extraordinary boy…
KISSTER: Boy
BOY
EXTRAORDINARY BOY
CANNAY: *(Emerging.)* Quiet, please –
KISSTER: This girl, in squirming to evade her destiny, has deliberately consigned herself to the tender mercies of a maniac –
GABRIELE: He is not a maniac –
KISSTER: A sportsman –
GABRIELE: He is not a sportsman –
KISSTER: A savage, a criminal –
GABRIELE: None of those things…!
CANNAY: Be quiet, I said –

KISSTER: And in the interests of civil order she must be constrained fetch ropes, handcuffs –

CANNAY: I will do no such thing –

KISSTER: Sedate her, then –

CANNAY: It's you who needs sedating –

KISSTER: It is, it is me, Gabriele –

CANNAY: CONTINUE YOUR DELIBERATIONS IN THE STREET, PLEASE...!
(Pause.)

KISSTER: *(To GABRIELE.)* How beautiful you are in black... when I possess you...the only colour you will wear will be –

GABRIELE: Never
Never
Will you possess me...
(CANNAY wheels away the body of COLOGNE.)

XII

GABRIELE: Never
Oh, can't you see the huge extent of never, Kisster?
(Pause...his eyes hang on hers...a man enters. GABRIELE extends an adoring hand to him.)

KISSTER: *(To the stranger.)* I put it to you...and Gabriele will confirm it...that being such a clever person...and accustomed to achieving his ends... I am now dangerously exposed to madness – not the clinical, not the decipherable sort of madness for which the world has devised so many practical solutions – but that other madness, not without its charm, which has recourse to grand religious or political –

RILEY: Savonarola...?
(Pause.)

KISSTER: Savonarola, for example –

RILEY: Luther...?
(Pause.)

KISSTER: Luther, too…

RILEY: Certainly one would not wish to see you driven into such a tortured deviancy –

KISSTER: With all its consequences –

RILEY: Its manifold and possibly infinite repercussions –
(A pause…they look at one another.)

RILEY: Go, now…
Turn your back on what cannot be yours…

GABRIELE: *(Not without tenderness.)* Go away, Kisster…

RILEY: Is that not the sign of a profound intelligence…?
(GABRIELE, adoring RILEY, cannot help herself kissing him.)

GABRIELE: I adore you…
(KISSTER watches their embrace.)
Oh, so adore you…
(KISSTER bites his lip in the horror of contemplation.)

KISSTER: This is probably worse – unquestionably worse – and worse in every way – than being beaten with a stick – for being beaten with a stick I was – whilst certainly in pain – at least conscious that I was the object of her passions – albeit passions of contempt – whereas the pain of this is unrelieved by any sense that she – even knows of my existence…

GABRIELE: Oh, so, oh, so adore…

KISSTER: And his advice was good, however tainted, stained, corroded by a triumphant masculinity, still it was good, and had I not been born under those specific circumstances that have made me what I am, I might well find myself persuaded, I might indeed respond to his finely-judged appeal to my intelligence, and turning my back –
(He is stopped by the spectacle of MENDEL, who rushes on the lovers brandishing a sword and with a single thrust, drives it through the bodies of both RILEY and GABRIELE so they stagger, pinned together and silent, fixed in their ordeal.)
Yes…!

Oh, yes…!
MY DARLING AND…
Oh, yes…!
OH GABR–IELE IS THAT DEATH…?
(They are still, upright, supported by one another.)
Gabriele…
(He peers tenderly at her.)
You are there…and I…
(He stares.)
am here…

MENDEL: She ridiculed us both…

KISSTER: Ridiculed…?

MENDEL: You and me both.

KISSTER: Certainly she deserved to die, then –
(MENDEL slaps KISSTER over the cheek. KISSTER nurses the place.)

MENDEL: I am going to the river –

KISSTER: The river, yes –

MENDEL: DON'T TRY TO DISSUADE ME…!

KISSTER: Was I?
Was I trying to dissuade you?

MENDEL: Telling me I might discover other life. What other life?

KISSTER: I don't know –

MENDEL: NO OTHER LIFE…!
(Pause… KISSTER is alarmed.)
And yet you have a point. Because if she defined the world, her absence must define it also…

KISSTER: Yes…

MENDEL: It is no less the world…!
(He looks about him, as if mesmerized.)
I merely fail to recognize it…
(Pause.)

KISSTER: Hence the river…

MENDEL: Don't keep on about the river –

KISSTER: I wasn't, I –

MENDEL: The world persists…! Is that not its crime…look, the sun…! The criminal sun…!

(KISSTER scrutinizes MENDEL, who smiles, benignly.)
Thank you…
I will give consideration to everything you say…
(He starts to go out, stops.)
For as she declared over and over again… Kisster
is a genius…and one must heed genius…even
when one recoils at what the genius has to say…
(He wanders away.)

KISSTER: She said that, did she…?
(MENDEL ignores him, goes out.)
She called me a genius…?
*(He observes the pierced couple, from whom blood
drips jointly into a pool…he is inexorably drawn to
the place…he kneels…he contemplates.)*
Oh, to be stabbed…
To be loved… and to be stabbed…
(The drips are loud as they fall into the pool.)
I was born at a roadside…and by a roadside I
shall die…
(He is still.)
By a roadside I shall die…
(He fails to die.)
I shall…
I SHALL DIE…
*(And fails still…his clenched fist drums the ground a
few times…he is aware of a figure watching him…it
is MARSTON.)*
The book I'm sorry to say the book through
no fault of my own on the contrary I struggled
to protect it the book is scattered to the four
corners of the earth and what a book it was
I endorse every sentence the angels hated it
and not just hated it the malice of those angels
the sheer undiluted malice I was bribed and
threatened swindled and cajoled –
*(MARSTON chucks down another. It lands with a slap.
Pause.)*
Oh, good, you had another…

(MARSTON drifts away… KISSTER climbs to his feet, picks up the book and is about to stuff it in a pocket when he chooses instead to cast a glance over it.)
'To Him For Whom the World – '
Hey…!
IT'S NOT THE SAME…!
(MARSTON has disappeared… KISSTER looks down at the book.)
'A Perfect Love' *(He flicks from page to page. He closes it with a finality, gripping it shut.)*
Everything's reversed…
(He knits his brows.)
Everything…
Reversed…
WHAT USE ARE YOU…?
(He puts the book, open, flat into the spreading pool of GABRIELE's blood…he works it backwards and forwards, as if he were scrubbing a floor with a brush. He wrings it out, like a washer-woman. He returns to his labour. He works his way over the stage. He disappears.)

CHRIST'S DOG

Characters

LAZAR
A Lover of Women, 65

BUDA
His Wife, 55

SISI
Another Wife, 35

BUBO
A Farmer, 40

MICHAEL
A Labourer

A SERVANT

CANAL
A Former Mistress, 40

JANUARY
An Athletic Husband, 30

TAX
A Son of Lazar, 23

FIRST RIVERMAN
A Collector of the Dead

SECOND RIVERMAN
A Collector of the Dead

MAN
A Passer-by

SMAJE
A Surgeon

TAWPAW
A Party-goer

NANA
A Party-goer

GUESTS
At a party

1

Snow falls on a ploughed field.
Three figures stagger with chairs. They sit. They gaze at the sky,
profoundly tired. Time elapses…

LAZAR: I burned my mouth
(Pause.)
I burned the roof of my mouth
(A wind passes over them.)
A thing I have not done for forty years it is
remarkable how rarely I have inflicted injury
upon myself razor cuts for example never have
I wounded myself shaving of how many men
could that be said very few I imagine or trapped
my finger in a door bruised my shins or even
stung myself on nettles it is a peculiar distinction
is it not others I have injured it goes without
saying but myself nothing nothing until today
what does that signify?
(The wind. LAZAR suddenly sits erect in the chair.)
I'm dying
(Pause.)
I'm dying what else is it I'm dying
(He looks to the motionless figures.)
I said I'm dying

BUDA: Lazar
(LAZAR emits a howl.)
Lazar you have burned the roof of your mouth
(He shakes his head bitterly.)
You swallowed hot coffee the coffee you
swallowed was certainly hot but was it boiling
no it was not
(He shakes it again.)
I joined you at breakfast I sat beside you you
may recollect and whereas the pot steamed this
steam was less an indication of the heat of the

191

coffee than the coldness of the room my breath
steamed also so did hers
(He shakes his head vehemently.)
It was a bitterly cold room in which to serve
breakfast
(He waves his arms in his frustration.)
Bitterly cold and the coffee was presumably
intended to compensate for this it was however
merely hot if it had ever boiled it boiled no
longer and whereas scalding of the mouth may
well be fatal to an infant you are not an infant
Lazar and you were not scalded far from dying
you are in perfect health
*(Pause. LAZAR, resigned, looks long and bitterly at
BUDA…)*

LAZAR: You are mundane you are mundane oh how
mundane you are mundane shallow and obtuse
did I say I was dying as a consequence of
swallowing hot coffee I did not everything you
have so meticulously and pedantically described
about breakfast coffee and the quality of the
hotel is beside the point the point being
(He loses patience with himself.)
oh
(He shrinks.)
oh
*(He lifts an arm, a gesture of futility, and lets it fall.
SISI rises from her chair and going to LAZAR, draws
up her coats and skirts to reveal her naked belly.
LAZAR lifts his head and contemplates her…)*
Piss now…

SISI: Can't

LAZAR: Piss…

SISI: Can't I said

LAZAR: Drink then you don't drink enough
*(SISI lets fall her clothing and returns to her chair…
Pause…)*

What I so obviously failed to elucidate with
regard to the burning of my mouth was the
sense that in my own case given the fastidious
manner in which I have conducted myself in
the world even a minor accident cannot be
consigned to the simply arbitrary character of
existence but must be viewed as a symptom
of altered conditions a harbinger of mortality
or if not mortality suffering am I exaggerating
I don't think so you know me you know how
I have lived tell me if I am exaggerating and
please please do not wilfully misunderstand me
not now not at this stage in our history I am
frightened it is not kind of you Buda

SISI: Buy me a drink and I'll drink it

BUDA: I apologize

LAZAR: I did not ask for an apology

BUDA: No but still I do apologize because I allowed my
irritation with your introspection to cause me to
patronize you to indulge my appetite for sarcasm
at your expense and so on it was infantile of
me I think perhaps I was myself frightened by
this unprecedented accident to your mouth and
refusing to acknowledge its significance took
refuge in mockery I dread your death you know
I do I have never known you harm yourself nor
even trip on a loose paving stone we must be
cautious now more cautious than we have ever
been

(LAZAR looks at her.)

LAZAR: But I am not cautious

(BUDA is embarrassed.)

BUDA: No

LAZAR: When was I ever cautious?

BUDA: Never Lazar

LAZAR: If caution had been a defining characteristic of
my life its immunity from accident would hardly
be extraordinary would it?

BUDA:	Not at all
LAZAR:	To describe my life as cautious diminishes me
BUDA:	Yes
LAZAR:	But perhaps that was your intention perhaps you entertain some secret longing to diminish me?
BUDA:	Not at all, Lazar
LAZAR:	Diminish if you wish but do not slander me
BUDA:	*(Protesting now.)* It was the wrong word, Lazar
LAZAR:	Yes
BUDA:	I picked a word the word was wrong but it's cold it's winter my blood is creeping and my brain is slow allow me one wrong word Lazar only one *(Pause.)* One *(Pause.)* One word? *(She glares at LAZAR.)* One? *(LAZAR concedes with a shrug.)*
LAZAR:	In any case the cautious I have observed are no less susceptible to accidents than the reckless
SISI:	*(Standing abruptly.)* I can now
LAZAR:	Their very fastidiousness exposes them to different but equally painful injuries
SISI:	All right?
LAZAR:	And please observe I do not stoop to include myself among the reckless
BUDA:	No indeed
LAZAR:	In denying I am cautious I should not want you to think I nourish some pitiful ambition to be classified among the daring
BUDA:	Impossible
LAZAR:	The brave or even God forbid the self-sacrificing
BUDA:	Impossible, Lazar
SISI:	I CAN I SAID
LAZAR:	*(Charmed.)* Piss then Piss for me

	(With an arrogant smile SISI strides to LAZAR and posing, jerks up her clothes. Hardly has she exposed herself than a shout travels over the landscape.)
SISI:	People
	(She drops her garments.)
	People
	(The cry is repeated. SISI returns to her chair, flings one leg over the other and looks discreetly at the ground.)
	People oh
	(The three stare at the earth. LAZAR plays with his fingers as three louts enter, armed and menacing...)
BUBO:	Whose field is this?
	(BUDA looks up, frowning...)
	Whose field I said? Who owns this field?
BUDA:	I couldn't say
BUBO:	You couldn't say? It's not you then, owns this field?
BUDA:	Me? No I don't own it
BUBO:	*(Indicating SISI.)* And her? Does she own it?
BUDA:	I don't think so, Sisi, do you own this field?
	(SISI giggles...)
	Not so far as we know
BUBO:	Not so far as you know she doesn't own it?
BUDA:	I say not so far as we know because property is a funny thing one day you have it and the next you don't I mean someone might die someone you never knew but who knew you dies and without saying a word they leave you property they leave you fields the first thing you know about it is a letter a letter comes from a solicitor and it lands on your mat it's not uncommon by not uncommon I mean I read about it once and then there are wars there are invasions you dig you plant year after year digging and planting you know the trees you know the birds you love the trees and birds and then over the horizon come oh it's terrible invaders that is

more common more common than letters from
solicitors you might say invaders are routine
(Pause.)

BUBO: You don't know who owns the field and you put
chairs on it
(BUDA bites her lip…)

BUDA: Small chairs…

BUBO: You put chairs in a field that does not belong
to you you sit on the chairs and you have
a conversation all three of you having a
conversation in a field that does not belong to
you am I right?
(Pause.)
AM I RIGHT OR AREN'T I?
(BUDA swallows nervously.)

BUDA: Apparently
(She perseveres.)
Apparently but this is interesting because it
is perfectly possible that this conversation we
were having, which was not a comfortable one,
was constrained by the very fact to which you
have drawn our attention, namely that we were
in ignorance as to whom the field belonged
yes in retrospect I'm certain the conversation
was profoundly influenced by this ignorance
and one might well generalize from this to say
of all conversations that they are qualitatively
altered improved or in this instance spoiled by
the critical fact as to whether one converses on
one's own land or whether one is technically a
trespasser …
(She pretends to smile… pause…)

BUBO: And then with complete disregard for the
ownership of the field she gets up this one she
gets up and
(He stops. He stares at SISI…)
with complete disregard…
(SISI shrugs…)

LAZAR:	Yes
	(The men do not remove their gaze from SISI…)
	Yes but that's to do with me
BUBO:	Shh
LAZAR:	It is entirely at my behest that she
BUBO:	Shh
LAZAR:	Does this
BUBO:	Shh
LAZAR:	This
BUDA:	Lazar shh
LAZAR:	BECAUSE SHE LOVES ME SHE
	(He stops, shrugs…)
	Does this
	(The men look at LAZAR, who stares at the ground a long pause…)
BUBO:	I'm a poor man
	(He looks at one of the others.)
	Poor as dirt isn't that so Michael that I'm a poor man dirt poor I am
MICHAEL:	He is
BUBO:	Tell these people how many fields I own Michael
	(MICHAEL laughs.)
	Tell them
MICHAEL:	One
BUBO:	Just one
MICHAEL:	He owns one field
BUBO:	This field and cloaks how many cloaks do I own Michael?
MICHAEL:	*(Mocking.)* Cloaks?
BUBO:	Yes how many cloaks?
MICHAEL:	No fucking cloaks
BUBO:	No cloaks but clocks how many clocks do I own tell them Michael please
MICHAEL:	No clocks or cloaks
BUBO:	And my kids how do they run about tell them Michael please how my children run about
MICHAEL:	WITH THEIR ARSES HANGING OUT

BUBO: *(Laughing with him.)* That's it that's it that's how
they run about
(A menacing pause elapses...)
Michael knows me you see
(The wind blows over them...)

LAZAR: I don't need this cloak...
(He looks at BUDA.)
Do I?
(BUDA lifts her shoulders...)
I can always get another cloak I

BUDA: *(Shaking her head at him.)* Shh

BUBO: *(To SISI.)* Over there you

BUDA: Now wait a minute

BUBO: OVER THERE BESIDE THE HEDGE YOU

BUDA: Wait I said

BUBO: *(Turning on BUDA.)* I WON'T WAIT NOT IN
MY OWN FIELD I WON'T WAIT DON'T
TELL ME TO WAIT IN MY OWN FIELD I'M
KING HERE IT'S MY KINGDOM WHY MY
KINGDOM I DIG IT THAT'S WHY I DIG
MY KINGDOM *(He glares. BUDA and LAZAR
visibly shrink...)*
Over there you
*(SISI is composed. She stands. She wipes her hands on
her skirts.)*

LAZAR: I'm her husband
(The wind blows...)
Please
(They stare at LAZAR, then idly push SISI off.)
She's my wife
*(They depart with SISI. BUDA and LAZAR remain
seated, their eyes fixed on one another...)*

BUDA: She'll be all right
(LAZAR gnaws his mouth.)
She'll be all right
*(SISI cries out distantly. LAZAR's face describes his
horror. A second cry follows...)*

(Affecting normality.) How's your mouth now? I
think looking back that coffee really was
(SISI cries out.)
boiling only I put milk in mine you know me I
never drink black coffee whereas you
(And again.)
And you came down before me only fractionally
but those few minutes make all the difference I'd
better look at it shall I look at it not that you can
do much with a burned mouth
(LAZAR opens his mouth.)
Now? Shall I look now?
(He gawps.)
Why not now yes I may as well look now I
*(She goes to rise off her chair, but is overcome by
a flood of tears. She falls back into her chair. Her
weeping echoes SISI's cries. LAZAR sits with his mouth
open. The contrasting cries of the women and the
wind together create a music to their pain. The third
man is discovered observing BUDA. She sees him. He
indicates with his thumb that she must go with him.
Her tears cease. She gets up to go. She looks at LAZAR,
and goes off. LAZAR, oblivious to his hanging mouth,
half-follows, stops, watches the events with a growing
fascination. He climbs unsteadily onto a chair…at last
BUBO returns. LAZAR defiantly remains on the chair.
BUBO collapses into another.)*

LAZAR: *(At last.)* Oh to be you…
(He covers his face with his hands.)
You ignorant and barbaric scum clawing your
one field with your fingers you clay-brain you
clay-arse dimly groping in the night for cunt and
teat the mongrels whining the cows splashing the
woman wet with sweat the woman slippery with
milk and frost in your arse-crack oh to be you
oh to be you and I have thirty thousand acres in
another country thirty thousand and a woman I

shall never enter oh to be you clay-mouth clay-
everything oh to be you…
*(LAZAR bites his lip. BUBO looks at him without
hatred. The other men return. BUBO stands and they
drift out. Suddenly MICHAEL returns and offers a
hand to LAZAR.)*
Thank you I am how sensitive you are how
intuitive of you to detect it I am accident-prone
*(He accepts MICHAEL's hand and steps off the chair.
MICHAEL goes out. LAZAR stares at the ground. He
pulls out a handkerchief and blows his nose. The
women enter, holding hands, also staring at the
ground. They look up at LAZAR simultaneously.
A burst of song.)*

*

2

A bed.
SISI enters, sees the bed and laughs.

BUBO: *(Entering.)* All I have all feel it the sheets the
pillowcases feel all I have feel it it's yours
(She laughs.)
Feel
Feel
(She shakes her head with contempt.)
All right don't feel look instead look at the labels
leave the labels on I said the tickets with the
prices leave them on
(She shakes her head and laughs.)
Look
Look
(She refuses.)
All right don't look listen forty thousand that
was the mattress
(He laughs now.)

Forty for the mattress forty I said what kind
of mattress could cost forty thousand I was
speechless only that he said that sort only he was
laughing at me you know the way they laugh
not open-mouthed but laughing all right I said
forty it is you bastard I did not say bastard Sisi
but I wanted to I rarely swear so that was the
mattress the head was eighty-seven eighty-seven
thousand and the foot was sixty add that up can
you add sixty to eighty-seven thousand I can
if you can't it's one hundred and forty-seven
thousand for the bed the bed alone or with the
mattress one hundred and eighty
(He falters.)
No yes one hundred and eighty-seven thousand
look for yourself I told them leave the labels on
(SISI is silent.)
Look at the labels look at the labels please
(She makes no move.)
I feel sick
(He chews. He swallows.)
So onto the linen the linen cost more than
the bed that isn't comprehensible I said that
bed linen should cost more than the bed that
depends on the linen she said it was a woman it
depends which linen and which bed I said I had
the most expensive bed in the whole city then it
deserves the most expensive linen she said I said
give it to me ninety thousand that was ninety
thousand for the linen and leave the labels on
I said I am buying the labels also the labels are
the evidence

SISI: Evidence?

BUBO: Of my sickness I am sick for you I had a farm I
had a wife undress get on the bed a small farm
and an ugly wife good riddance to the farm
good riddance to the wife undress I said undress
and kids good riddance to them too it's you I

love undress undress or I will do something so
terrible to you undress please please undress or
don't undress dressed or undressed I don't care
lie there lie there

*(He squirms. He weeps. He is sick. SISI observes his
ordeal. At last she goes to him, and standing above
him, draws his head into her skirts. She strokes his
hair as a mother comforts a child. LAZAR enters.)*

LAZAR: The death of a great man

(He flops onto the bed.)

and I don't say I'm great poses the worst
dilemma of his entire existence obviously he
wants to die with dignity one might say the
moral arithmetic of his whole being urges
him to succeed in this as in nothing else but
where are his resources death consists precisely
in the abolition of those resources he has
so assiduously accumulated in his life every
stratagem is ridiculed every gesture mocked by
physical decay prop the pillows prop them

BUDA: *(Entering.)* You are not dying

SISI: *(As BUBO wails.)* Shh shh

LAZAR: And how necessary this is how necessary that he
be exposed to the squalor of his new condition
and reconciled to it only by conceding however
reluctantly that the only relief from the sordid
experience of dying is death itself can he be
persuaded to so to speak walk through that door

SISI: *(To BUBO.)* Shh shh

LAZAR: It is after all the only door the whole idea of the
perfect death is therefore contradictory pillows
pillows please the fact is that if the act of dying
were susceptible to dignity one would never die
I say the act of dying it is death that acts

SISI: *(Abandoning BUBO.)* You are not dying

BUDA: So I keep telling him

SISI: *(Adjusting her hat, as BUBO wails.)* Oh shut up do

BUDA:	No one who talks this much is dying I have been with dying people and they don't talk like this
LAZAR:	You generalize
BUDA:	Do I?
LAZAR:	It has always been the weakest aspect of your reasoning
BUDA:	Has it good
LAZAR:	I cannot tell you how over the years this tendency to generalize has irritated my nerves
BUDA:	Tell me tell me now
LAZAR:	I will do now is the time to tell you obviously
BUBO:	*(Getting up off the floor.)* My bed
LAZAR:	The fact is our intellectual companionship profound as it has been was always compromised by this peculiar form of idleness
BUBO:	*(Seeing LAZAR lying there.)* My bed
LAZAR:	For that is what it is
BUDA:	*(Defiantly.)* Is it
LAZAR:	Moral idleness
BUDA:	Thank you
LAZAR:	You asked and I have told you pillows please for the third time
BUBO:	*(Staring in disbelief.)* My bed
LAZAR:	There is a condition of morbidity which induces the most intense illumination both of thought and articulation I have it
BUDA:	Possibly
LAZAR:	Certainly I have it
BUBO:	HE IS IN MY BED
SISI:	It is not your bed
BUBO:	WHOSE BED IS IT THEN
SISI:	Mine it is my bed you gave it to me
BUBO:	I gave it to you yes
SISI:	So it is my bed
BUBO:	TO LOVE ME IN
SISI:	You are such a baby really such a baby such a such a baby kiss me
BUBO:	No

	(SISI shrugs.)
LAZAR:	*(To BUBO.)* A present is a present it cannot carry obligations with it surely or it becomes a bribe a present has no policy
BUBO:	SHUT UP
LAZAR:	Arguably
BUBO:	SHUT UP
LAZAR:	There has never in all of human history been a present therefore
BUDA:	Shh
LAZAR:	Arguably
BUBO:	I want to kill him
SISI:	Silly
BUBO:	I WANT TO KILL ALL OF YOU
SISI:	Silly
LAZAR:	Yes it is silly

(SISI cries suddenly.)

And now you have made Sisi cry she loves me
and hates all killing Sisi Sisi he does not mean a
word he says

(She flings herself in LAZAR's arms, sobbing…)

Love her love her if you love her she will love
you isn't that what you want?

(BUBO shakes his head angrily.)

You don't want to be loved by Sisi?

(BUBO grunts bitterly.)

There is nothing like it nothing in the world
she clings she draws her man into the middle of
her heart and he swims there I have been with
seven hundred women and only Sisi took me
swimming in her heart's blood only Sisi but you
know this I saw I watched it from my chair the
wind blew chill your ugly arse was bare at first
she wept and then slowly her knees came up
her feet fixed on you like a marriage a hare was
passing did I say this Buda the hare stopped rose
and stared it knew the miracle of Sisi

(Pause…)

BUBO:	I own the bitch
LAZAR:	You do you do own her pillows please
	(BUDA arranges the pillows behind LAZAR.)
	But to be loved where you own oh
SISI:	*(Removing herself from LAZAR's embrace.)* Shh
	Shh
LAZAR:	You owned the field Mr Bubo but did it love you?
SISI:	Shh
LAZAR:	I am reminding Mr Bubo of the extent of his privilege a privilege which to judge by his routine itemizing of his sacrifices his ugly wife his sterile cow
BUDA:	Lazar
LAZAR:	His sickly infants and his fallow field he is only dimly aware of
BUDA:	Lazar
LAZAR:	*(Undeterred.)* This exquisite woman formerly a dancer formerly the mistress of not one but two princes of obscure kingdoms and currently the wife of yes yes let us not baulk at the word the wife of a genius has in the mysterious way of women fallen in love with the brute who violated her in a sodden field and welcomes him yes when we articulate a thing it becomes yet more extraordinary welcomes him into her womb and he is a spectacle of such unmitigated ignorance he cannot even grasp the scale of his good fortune
BUDA:	Shh now
LAZAR:	So I am telling him
BUDA:	Yes
LAZAR:	I am educating Mr Bubo in the subtle and arcane science
BUDA:	Yes
LAZAR:	Of knowing a good thing when he sees it
	(SISI bursts out laughing.)
BUBO:	*(Wounded.)* I will smack him in a minute

LAZAR: Smack me yes I'm dying
SISI: *(Jumping off the bed and glaring at BUBO.)* You
            smack him and I'll smack you
LAZAR: A dying man requires a smack to help him on
            his way
BUDA: You are not dying Lazar
            (SISI and BUBO spontaneously embrace.)
LAZAR: Rather as a mule that is reluctant to go into its
            stable submits more swiftly to a blow
BUDA: Shut up about dying
LAZAR: Than any amount of argument
BUDA: *(At the end of her patience.)* Oh just shut up and
            you
            *(She turns to address BUBO, who has drawn SISI to
            the floor.)*
            Oh
LAZAR: Smack smack
BUDA: *(Sitting wearily on the bed.)* Oh
LAZAR: *(Amused.)* Smack smack
            (Pause. A miasma of despair settles over BUDA.)
BUDA: You swallowed my life oh I had a life and you
            swallowed it I don't think I was even chewed
            was I was I chewed I don't remember any
            chewing what was there to chew everything
            you uttered became a song for me the more
            preposterous your ideas the more they appealed
            to me theft murder bigamy I sang I sang it
            all but it's time to go I want one room with
            a window-box I'm fifty-seven there might be
            something which is not Lazar in me I don't
            know a little that is not Lazar I don't know but
            I want to see Sisi will organize your funeral
            goodbye don't argue
            (BUDA stands.)
            Goodbye
            *(She walks out swiftly. LAZAR is still. SISI moans on
            the floor. A SERVANT enters with a towel and a razor.
            He goes to LAZAR and prepares him.)*

SERVANT: Life dies…
             (He lathers expertly.)
             Life dies…
             (SISI emits a deep sob.)
             And in another place…
             (And again.)
             Life lives…
LAZAR: Not always in the same room
SERVANT: Not always in the same room no but you seem
             to make the world disclose itself more brutally
             than some would wish if I may say so my Lord
             you provoke it it loses its dignity and like an
             old maid who has drunk too much it begins to
             blaspheme horribly I always thought my Lord
             Lazar was too clever for the world the world
             is embarrassed by him its crude mechanisms
             its banal appetites he mocks them with his
             sophistication what can the world do to smother
             its shame only punish him but how it is a
             problem inventing punishment for such a man
             as you death is oh so obvious death is
             (He wields the razor with infinite skill.)
             In many ways I think
             (He wipes the blade.)
             The world being childish
SISI: *(Pushing away BUBO and swiftly rising.)* Sorry
             (LAZAR lifts a hand like a blessing.)
             Sorry I
             (He repeats the gesture.)
             WHAT AM I SORRY FOR?
             (She looks at the SERVANT.)
             And he should shave his face is like a crop of
             thistles
             (She nurses her chin.)
             Shave him will you?
             *(She goes out. Her loud weeping is suddenly heard
             from outside.)*
LAZAR: *(Consoling her.)* Sisi

	Sisi *(She runs back in and flings herself in LAZAR's arms. The SERVANT makes way for her, his razor in the air…)*
SISI:	I love him
LAZAR:	Yes
SISI:	I love him
LAZAR:	You do it's curious but you do
SISI:	Is it curious I don't know yes it is it is curious explain it for me I can't explain it for me Lazar please
BUBO:	*(Threatening the SERVANT.)* If I want a shave I'll say so me *(The SERVANT inclines his head.)* Two hundred and seventy-seven thousand and I fuck on the floor two hundred and seventy-seven thousand it hurts it hurts
SISI:	He's dying, Bubo
BUBO:	Let him die on the floor I'm sorry but it hurts
SISI:	You are a pig Bubo what a pig you are
BUBO:	I am
SISI:	A pig and a horse and a
BUBO:	I am all those things
SISI:	A horse and a bull and a pig and a and a
BUBO:	Sisi
SISI:	Pig and a pig and a
BUBO:	Sisi I will break your jaw *(The SERVANT seizes BUBO and thrusts him out of the door. A tumult of fighting and shouting ensues on the stairs and in the street…)*
LAZAR:	*(In the returned silence.)* His semen swims his semen swims in Sisi frantic and alive…
SISI:	I'll piss for you
LAZAR:	It swims
SISI:	I will Lazar
LAZAR:	It swims
SISI:	I love you do you see I love you Lazar let me piss for you please

(LAZAR looks into SISI. He frowns. He emits a deep cry…now she comforts him…)
Shh
Oh shh

*

3

BUDA with a pot of geraniums. An elegant woman appears.

BUDA: Lazar is dying
            (Pause.)
            Lazar is dying and I have a room
            (Pause.)
            For thirty years I wanted to leave Lazar why not
            wait another week I don't know perhaps I have
            a longing to be cruel perhaps his decay disgusts
            me it's small my room but Lazar is not in it how
            wonderful that is he is not there and soon yes
            soon he will be nowhere wonderful wonderful
            I have not been so happy since I was a child it
            is revenge perhaps yes certainly it is revenge I
            shall never see Lazar again never never let him
            cry out for me it started with a burn he burned
            his mouth I knew at once something profoundly
            serious has occurred it won't be me he cries out
            for will it it will be you
            (Pause. She shows the geraniums.)
            For the window-box
            (She laughs.)
            He never mentions you by name but why else
            would he come here why this city and no other
            we walked we had no money for the train we
            carried three chairs and a suitcase twice we
            were robbed and twice the thieves came after us
            apologizing I say three chairs Lazar has a new
            wife yes another one a dancer a farmer raped

her in a field they fell in love the police were no
different to the thieves one minute they were
putting handcuffs on him the next they brought
him cups of tea it's his face isn't it it's Lazar's
face it lingers in the memory it's ethical it's holy
it's a mask of human tenderness and spirituality
but you can have too much of a good thing
when they had finished raping her they turned
to me same men same field it was snowing she
hasn't danced for years now something in her
knee snowing yes pretty in its own way
*(She comes to a stop. The woman looks at BUDA
a long time. A man enters. He kisses the woman
lingeringly, then parts. Together they look at BUDA.)*

CANAL: I married again

BUDA: *(Cheerfully.)* So much marriage marriage
everywhere and they say it's out of date
personally I long for solitude mice doves and
a window box I can give you Lazar's address
it's squalid obviously a dirty room on the fifth
floor somehow they got a bed in it you don't like
dirt do you me neither the room is dirty but the
bed's in cellophane do you want the address?
(CANAL only looks.)
Do you want the address this pot is heavy all
right you don't want it poor Lazar poor Lazar
(She shakes her head…)
Good however yes it's good in many ways it is
good to discover even on the point of death that
no one can have it all his own way spiritual faces
so what ethical expressions
(She pretends to laugh.)
Lovely for a day or two but we know you and I
we know don't we
*(The pot of geraniums falls from BUDA's arms and
crashes to the floor. There is a fractional silence, then
the man erupts.)*

JANUARY: Excellent excellent his dying excellent the dying
          of a liar a sadist and a thief I never knew the
          man but excellent excellent his dying let him
          turn on his agony like meat roasting on a spit
          drip drip the criminal drip drip the hypocrite
          slow dying I never knew the man but the slowest
          of all dying let us hope for it I'll get a dustpan
          (He walks out. CANAL looks at BUDA. She lifts her
          hands in a gesture. JANUARY returns with a dustpan
          and broom. He crouches at BUDA's feet.)
          I never knew the man but I don't need to know
          him she knows him show your body show the
          map of your ordeal knifescars burnscars head
          to toe I exaggerate but hardly do I I hardly
          exaggerate
          (He rises, tapping the broom on the pan. He looks at
          BUDA.)
          Thank you for delivering the inspiring and
          gratifying news of the mortal sickness of a liar
          (BUDA is laughing.)
          a sadist and a hypocrite
          (CANAL laughs also.)
          Yes yes rejoice
          (He pretends to share their humour.)
          I am opening a bottle I am I am I AM
          OPENING A BOTTLE
          (He is faintly bewildered. He hesitates…)

CANAL: *(Her eyes fixed on BUDA.)* Who's stopping you?
          (JANUARY flinches.)

JANUARY: No one no one's stopping me
          (He hurries out. A pause…)

CANAL: Idiot
          (BUDA laughs…)
          Ox-brained idiot Lazar said it's perfectly all right
          to torture idiots so I married him Lazar tortured
          me of course I don't mean cuts I don't mean
          burns

BUDA: No

CANAL: The cuts and burns I asked for
BUDA: Yes
CANAL: *(Laughing.)* Asked for? I pleaded
            (They smile. CANAL bites her lip.)
            He won't come back all that about the bottle
            he won't come back if he has one redeeming
            quality it is that he has second thoughts his first
            thoughts are ugly ugly always he is lying on
            the bed now weeping weeping with his second
            thoughts it's all right it's perfectly all right did
            you like him go to him if you want to it's the
            third door on the left you'll hear him weeping
            (BUDA is mildly surprised. CANAL shrugs...)
            I can't see Lazar
BUDA: No
CANAL: *(Turning.)* I can't I can't see Lazar
            *(She briskly leaves. BUDA hesitates. She is about
            to go herself when JANUARY enters holding a pot
            of geraniums identical to the broken one. He stands
            before BUDA, staring at the floor. BUDA goes to receive
            the flowers but JANUARY holds the pot firmly in two
            hands.)*
JANUARY: Not a gift
            (Pause.)
BUDA: Not a gift?
            (JANUARY is silent.)
            I see
JANUARY: You have been with Lazar
BUDA: Thirty years yes thirty years with him
JANUARY: Lazar says nothing is free I quote Lazar
BUDA: You quote him correctly
            *(At last JANUARY lifts his eyes to BUDA. They
            comprehend.)*
            You carry them you carry them home for me
            (She turns and leaves. He follows.)

                  *

4

The bed.
LAZAR draped with SISI, who sleeps.

CANAL: I came as soon as I could no I didn't I could
have come sooner I made up my face not
only that I didn't have the lipstick finding it
the one you liked the one you always insisted
on took three-quarters of an hour two shops
no three three shops it was so I might have
been three-quarters of an hour sooner with a
plain face washed of course but plain now tell
me you dislike this colour tastes change but I
had nothing to go on but my memory of your
inflexibility you smacked me once in public for
altering the shade of it my lipstick smacked me
in a café for trying out a different shade and I
did it to please you the shock of it caused me to
drop my bag the contents rolled over the tiles
people went on hands and knees collecting them
how moved they were by pity and by rage the
tears stood in my eyes they wanted to take me to
bed they wanted to demonstrate their spiritual
superiority I did not cry out loud abandon the
temperamental idiot they longed to say I did not
abandon you
(Pause.)

LAZAR: Sisi
(LAZAR shakes her gently by the shoulder.)
This is Sisi
(SISI rubs her eyes.)
Sisi show your mouth
(She lifts her face to LAZAR.)
Not to me to her
(Puzzled, SISI looks to CANAL. CANAL laughs.)
Yes
Yes

SISI: *(Chagrined.)* What's funny?

LAZAR: Is it not hilarious the conviction I bring to my erotic principles?

SISI: *(Jumping off the bed.)* What's funny I said?

LAZAR: *(As CANAL laughs.)* My unswerving loyalty to a handful of fixed ideas?

           (SISI pulls a hand-mirror from her pocket and examines herself.)

           Was ever a man more passionate in his principles was ever a man?

SISI: *(Seeing CANAL's face over the rim.)* That's my lipstick…

LAZAR: In this respect and this alone Lazar was a narrow-minded bigot flame-red hell-fire scarlet-woman rouge-de-biche nothing changes but the names as for clothes

SISI: *(Laughing now.)* My lipstick…!

LAZAR: Black only only black wardrobe upon wardrobe of black clothes it was as if Lazar from his youth even obliged his mistresses to rehearse his funeral

CANAL: Why do you talk of yourself in the past tense?

SISI: He does that now he does it all the time don't you?

LAZAR: *(Undeviating.)* Might it not be argued however that the very rigidity of Lazar's ideas with regard to the appearance of his mistresses was testament to the profound fascination they held for him and evidence his appetite required none of that stimulation conventionally provided by the thing called fashion what is fashion after all?

CANAL: Lazar…

LAZAR: What is it but the failure of desire made into art?

CANAL: Lazar…

LAZAR: Lazar did not need fashion because in Lazar desire never failed…

SISI: Bubo says that Bubo says the money women waste on clothes

LAZAR: Sisi…
SISI: It's outrageous Bubo says
LAZAR: Sisi never speak of Lazar in the same breath as
              Bubo no opinion entertained by Bubo could
              possibly accord with mine in any case I do not
              have opinions Bubo has opinions and what I
              have just elucidated is so remote from Bubo's
              pitiful
              (He waves an arm impatiently.)
              Oh never mind…
CANAL: Lazar you are not dying are you you are merely
              talking of yourself in the past tense you are
              entertaining the idea of your immortality Buda
              was wrong this past tense this third person it's a
              it's a I don't know it's
              (She shakes her head.)
              an affectation and I spent three-quarters of an
              hour looking for this lipstick
LAZAR: Why?
CANAL: Why?
LAZAR: Why yes why march the damp streets looking
              for a lipstick of such moral and historical
              significance did you imagine it would comfort a
              dying man to expire in a cloud of reminiscences
              or was it to torture him to make his last hours
              swarm with fevers imagining who enjoyed that
              red mouth now I detest you I always detested
              you and when I did not detest you I was bored
              by you slap my face Canal what is twenty
              years to wait for the incomparable pleasures of
              revenge and Buda is not incorrect I am dying
              but I am dying at my own behest you must all
              be patient and death he must learn patience too
              Sisi ask Bubo to throw this woman out of here if
              he would be so kind he owes me a favour
              *(A pause of despair. SISI and CANAL are both
              shaken… CANAL shakes her head.)*

My hatred for you if you can imagine it has on
seeing you grown more intense find Bubo drag
Bubo out of whatever cellar he is drinking in
tell him I require a little of his violence say it's a
woman he will come he likes women
(SISI dithers.)
FETCH BUBO
(SISI goes out.)
In his own fashion he likes women I don't
criticize the many ways in which women may be
liked let the women criticize

CANAL: Yes

LAZAR: Let the women say his liking is a liking I don't
like

CANAL: Yes

LAZAR: The women will the women will say it

CANAL: Yes

LAZAR: That I like

CANAL: And that I do not like Lazar I suffered you for
seven years

LAZAR: *(Fatigued.)* Please

CANAL: Seven years liking what I did not like

LAZAR: Please

CANAL: Terribly loving and terribly disliking

LAZAR: *(Vehemently.)* If there is one and only one
privilege which must be accorded to the dying
it is surely this that they are delivered from the
repetition of the grievances of the living the half-
living and the so-called living who cares what
you disliked you loved love neither likes nor
dislikes it is love

CANAL: Lazar

LAZAR: And love

CANAL: Lazar

LAZAR: LOVE IS UNCONDITIONAL
(CANAL seems exhausted…)

CANAL: Forgive Lazar forgive yourself and forgive me
(LAZAR smiles thinly.)

LAZAR: Forgiveness…
            (Pause.)
            To forgive is to be ashamed of the anger the
            offence gave rise to never will I demean our love
            by forgiving you I hate you and why you wear
            the lipstick of our agony I do not know except to
            make more agony
            *(He shakes his head now. CANAL's shoulders heave
            with her uncontrollable grief.)*
            I must get up
            (He moves stiffly.)
            I must
            (He winces with pain.)
            no matter what it takes
            (He swings his legs over the side of the bed.)
            disassociate myself from this
            (He stands. He sways.)
            parody of a deathbed scene Sisi
            (He grabs a bedpost.)
            Sisi who is not sophisticated
            (He steadies himself.)
            even Sisi will find herself unable to govern her
            talent for mockery it is arguably
            (He straightens himself.)
            the only talent Sisi has and I do not wish to
            encourage it no not the only talent she is a
            brilliant mimic also and I have no doubt the
            explanation for the inordinate delay in her
            reappearing with Bubo to fling you into the
            street is that she is entertaining some gang of
            drunken louts with comic renderings of your
            walk your voice your syntax etcetera pity Sisi I
            do she so wants to be cruel

CANAL: *(Wiping her eyes.)* Why did you come here?
LAZAR: *(Looking at BUBO's bed.)* I never liked beds
CANAL: Why Lazar?
LAZAR: Neither to sleep nor fuck in the chair on the
            other hand the chair oh

(Irritated, CANAL goes to leave.)
the infinite utility of the chair I DON'T KNOW
WHY
(CANAL stops.)
Why would a man deliver himself to the
torture of your proximity only surely out of
some forlorn hope he might discover he had
developed in the fifteen years of silence an
exquisite immunity feeling nothing nothing
any more but astonishment he had shared an
intimacy with you in the first place yes that
might be the reason but I don't know Lazar
Lazar is a mystery to me…
(Their eyes meet…)

CANAL: And did he did Lazar find himself immune to
me I have a husband did I say a husband Lazar
half my age an ox with ox's thighs arsed like an
ox and with an ox's nervous eye I scarcely need
to move he charges me five six seven times a
day I find myself sitting in cafés not looking for
a man Lazar but seeking relief from one is Lazar
immune I came to make him say he loved me
with his last breath but Lazar is not dying is he
not today?
(LAZAR regards her…)
Neither dying nor immune?
*(She laughs mildly, dragging up her skirt with one
hand. LAZAR stares at her exposed nakedness. They
are still. A profound despair overcomes LAZAR. A man
enters. He perches at the foot of the bed, and pulls off
one shoe…)*

TAX: Christ had a dog…
(Then the other…)
How many people know that?
(He lays back over the bed, gazing at the ceiling.)
It wasn't that he wanted the dog the dog
followed him whether it was a mongrel or a
pedigree no one knows…

(CANAL drops her skirts…)
I think it was pure-bred myself and highly-
strung the more he tried to lose it the more it
clung to him naturally he was embarrassed there
was no room in that troubled head of his for
trivial sentiments such as we feel for cats and
parrots and in a way it made a fool of him the
disciples sensed this they were all for drowning
it but if Christ countenanced the murder of an
inoffensive animal what would that say about his
famous pity he had a dilemma on his hands and
it was a mischievous animal mischievous and
loyal the loyalty he could hardly object to but
the mischief…
(Pause.)
Oh the mischief…
(Pause. He sits up.)
I hate you so do many others they cannot all be
here I speak for them however tell this woman
go now and the one smoking at the bottom of
the stairs now please
*(LAZAR makes a sign with his head. CANAL is
unwilling to concede. She glares at TAX…)*
I heard your cries I smelled your odours in
my father's hair his lip was moist from your
own moisture and when he placed a finger on
the open pages of my schoolbook I stared to
see what stain it left the colour of your womb
on Horace or on Tacitus so you see we are
acquainted my poor mother please my poor
mother please
*(Pause. CANAL strides from the room… LAZAR shifts
uncomfortably…TAX emits a long and agonized howl.
The bed sinks out of sight…)*

*

5

A tomb by a great river.
LAZAR enters on his stick. TAX follows at a distance carrying a chair.
LAZAR observes the tomb dispassionately.

LAZAR: *(At last.)* I don't apologize
(Pause.)
Never have I apologized it is the first law of my life
(Pause.)
On the other hand I lie
(Pause.)
Always I have lied it is the second law so
(He makes a gesture of a futility.)
I might apologize in order to satisfy you but what meaning would it have?
(TAX is bitter, silent. LAZAR walks to the riverbank.)
Your mother loved the river but not the chemicals that contaminate it it grieved her that the water changes colour all the time I said I found it beautiful for daring to express this heresy she called me *contrary* because my tastes so rarely accord with the majority *contrary* as if it were an affectation on my part *contrary* poor-minded was your mother and she used poor words
(He opens his hands.)
there
(He shrugs his shoulders.)
now I have issued a damning verdict on her and you commanded me to grieve I have not been here since the funeral as your surmised chair now give me the chair
(TAX coldly unfolds the chair and places it for LAZAR, who sits, staring out. Pause…)

TAX: Christ tolerated the dog he did not love it nor did he feed it others did nevertheless its loyalty

was to him always it brought to him the pitiful
fragments of its mischief laying at the feet of him
who was pure in heart the evidence of its own
impurity it has to be said Christ was not in the
dog nor was the dog in Christ all the same they
trod the same road even to Calvary it howled
it howled at Calvary the soldiers drove it away
with stones yet it came back howling none of
this is mentioned in the scriptures nor does any
painting show Christ's dog there are powerful
reasons for this omission obviously
(Pause. LAZAR turns to TAX.)

LAZAR: Undress a woman young or old undress her and
wonder
(TAX seems to meditate on this proposal.)

TAX: Yes
(He bites his lip.)
I could do that no son of yours could possibly
have failed to register the fascination that
attaches to undressing do I sound sarcastic?

LAZAR: *(With deliberation.)* Or better still

TAX: I am sarcastic

LAZAR: Cause the woman to undress herself

TAX: Deeply sarcastic

LAZAR: Obviously this undressing is for you but it must
include her own pleasure if she feels no pleasure
in her nakedness the nakedness becomes a gift

TAX: More sarcastic than I can say

LAZAR: And gifts oh gifts what are they but the murder
of desire?
(They stare at one another.)
I should like you to meet Sisi

TAX: *(Wildly gesticulating to the tomb.)* MY MOTHER'S
GRAVE

LAZAR: Yes

TAX: In the field of suicides my mother's grave
(His hand hangs in the air. Pause…)

LAZAR: With Sisi nothing is without its ambiguities Sisi is a dancer
(The hand falls…)
In relation to a dancer whilst there is no kindness in her nakedness there is no innocence in it either always the invisible hand of the public disposes her limbs there is a body in the water a body coming in
(He looks at the river…)

TAX: The bend…

LAZAR: The bend yes…

TAX: *(Hurrying down.)* No corpse can pass the bend

LAZAR: This simplifies life for the authorities

TAX: *(Calling.)* IT'S A WOMAN

LAZAR: As for the suicides they derive some satisfaction from knowing their destination I daresay
(A cry from TAX as he wades in…)
And it's picturesque here the trees the birds the sun setting beneath the bridges
(TAX cries out again…)
It's a positive inducement I can't help you I'm dying
(TAX is struggling and weeping simultaneously.)
A woman is it?
(TAX wails.)
Young or old?

TAX: *(Bitterly.)* I don't know…

LAZAR: Look at her

TAX: I am looking at her

LAZAR: Look at her neck is her neck young or old?
(TAX sobs.)
Look I said

TAX: *(Provoked.)* You look
(TAX stands holding up SISI's arms by the wrists. LAZAR struggles to climb off the chair. He makes his way to the water's edge…)
Oh what makes a woman kill herself?

	(He sobs as he struggles to hold the body in the current.)
LAZAR:	Only a man
TAX:	*(Struggling.)* I hate you I hate you
LAZAR:	It might be debt it might be sickness but what is sickness if you have a man what is debt to the well-loved if it is not a man it is the absence of one lift her head for me lift it lift it
TAX:	*(Fighting the river.)* How can I
LAZAR:	*(Staring at the body.)* Lift it lift it you scum
TAX:	I hate you father
LAZAR:	You filth you scum lift it
TAX:	Oh how I hate you
LAZAR:	*(In his extremity.)* LIFT LIFT
TAX:	I CAN'T I CAN'T
	(A bell is rung along the shore. LAZAR is quite still, TAX holds on. An appalling pause as the river runs on and LAZAR stares. He returns agonized to his chair. A cry at a distance…)
LAZAR:	*(Seated.)* Sorry
	(TAX fixes himself in the mud, grasping the body of SISI, his eyes closed.)
	Sorry
RIVERMAN:	*(Calling.)* COMING TO YOU
LAZAR:	I used words then I rarely use obviously there are better words
RIVERMAN:	*(Calling.)* COMING TO YOU
LAZAR:	But at that moment I could not find the better words unusual for me unusual sorry
	(Two RIVERMEN enter, one pushing a handcart. They go at once into the water, relieving TAX, who sobs as he climbs up the bank. LAZAR offers a hand to his son but TAX shakes his head. He sits heavily on the ground, head in hands…)
FIRST R'MAN:	My girl I say even if they are not girls I say my girl even at seventy my girl I say always they come from hard men's hands my girl my girl I have a way with them it is as if they come back

	to their father and he washes them the girls come home to be washed
LAZAR:	*(Standing.)* I'll wash this one
FIRST R'MAN:	*(As they deposit the body on the cart.)* I wash my girls it's what they pay me for
LAZAR:	I'll pay you more
TAX:	*(Horrified.)* What? *(He scrambles up.)* What? What are you saying?
LAZAR:	*(To the RIVERMEN.)* A sponge a hairbrush and a clean towel please
SECOND R'MAN:	He never lets a stranger near his girls
LAZAR:	Never obviously and soap also did I say soap?
TAX:	*(Passionately.)* Let a poor girl lie in her death let her hide inside her silence what are you a dog?
LAZAR:	*(To the RIVERMEN.)* My son
TAX:	A hyena a crow a carrion crow? *(As the SECOND R'MAN goes out.)* Don't go don't go
FIRST R'MAN:	*(To TAX.)* This place please this place please it isn't any place this place
TAX:	I know my mother's there *(He jabs his finger towards the tomb. Pause.)*
FIRST R'MAN:	My girls I think how loud the city is with girls my girls laughing my girls loving hard men's hands I wait like an anxious father *(He looks at the body of SISI.)* Lipstick *(He shakes his head, going out as the SECOND RIVERMAN returns with a bucket, sponge, soap and towel. He places the items on the ground. TAX seems to want to admonish him, but he also withdraws. Instead he goes to address LAZAR.)*
LAZAR:	*(Pitifully.)* Sisi *(TAX is aghast. LAZAR turns his head to his son.)* Sisi *(LAZAR's hands grope the air…)*
TAX:	*(Going to the handcart.)* This is Sisi?

(He stares at the corpse.)

Your wife Sisi?

LAZAR: I married her but I was already married so she never was my wife under the law what's more I never entered her she pissed for me she kissed and pissed I call that love other men they other men lots of other men they did what I

(He shrugs pitifully.)

Wife to me however wife to me

TAX: Two wives

(He lifts his hands in disbelief.)

Two wives in this little sea of

LAZAR: Three

(Pause.)

TAX: Three?

(LAZAR picks up the bucket and goes to the cart. He gazes at SISI's corpse.)

Three?

(LAZAR wrings out the sponge and begins to wash SISI's face.)

Three who is the other does it matter three three suicides the other who was she three suicides and in a single river there are many rivers so there are presumably more suicides are there more tell me stop sponging her face it is a fiction a fiction of grief a self-indulgence a preposterous mockery put down the sponge I'll kill you I have always wanted to kill you are you conscious of this longing in me murderer?

(LAZAR stops sponging. He looks to TAX.)

LAZAR: Sisi…

TAX: Sisi no liar Sisi no

(TAX grabs the bucket from LAZAR's hands and in his rage flings it away into the river. A pause, then TAX weeps bitterly.)

Who could stand here and not kill you who it is incomprehensible to me the fact you have never yet been killed incomprehensible

LAZAR:	It's my face
TAX:	*(Violently.)* SHE HAS A FACE SHE HAS A FACE A VASTLY BETTER FACE THAN YOU
LAZAR:	Indisputably
TAX:	Sisi
	(He shakes his head.)
	Sisi
	(LAZAR is bemused to see TAX go to the body and lifting her shoulders smother her face in kisses. He observes this for a moment, then goes to the tomb and runs his head over its surfaces…)
LAZAR:	I had money then
	(TAX sobs…)
	Architects sculptors stonemasons all the latest in memorial design urns drapes tablets marbles from Sicily bits of English iron there was a book I pointed to the items that that and that the cost oh never mind the cost I liked grand gestures I was young they piled it on a forest in Bohemia so what a lead-mine I thought grief rather suited me and the women oh the women and with this orphaned boy both of us white as snow they were desperate to console me oh desperate *(LAZAR does not observe SISI's arms slowly enclose TAX in an embrace…)* Did any woman know Lazar I don't think so and he liked lying even in deep nakedness even in the mirrored halls of pure gaze he had to hide concealment was a passion with him no wonder so many died it's hard for women they think inside them you are briefly innocent but no I stood against the womb and still I lied not Sisi Sisi I *(He sees SISI and TAX silently adoring.)* Sisi I never visited

(He gazes, disbelieving…rain falls…a figure passes with an umbrella…)

I'm dying fetch me the chair…

(The figure ignores him. Thunder, and the rhythm of rain in the river. SISI laughs in her pleasure… LAZAR takes a step nearer…another figure enters with an umbrella.)

I'm dying fetch me the chair…

(The figure passes. A pause, then LAZAR edges nearer the handcart, mesmerized. A third figure appears, also with an umbrella. LAZAR does not look at him.)

Fetch me the chair I'm

(SISI and TAX whisper and giggle. The figure stops, but LAZAR is too preoccupied with the spectacle of the lovers to notice…)

RIVERMEN: *(Distantly.)* OI

LAZAR: Chair…

RIVERMEN: OI

LAZAR: *(His arm groping.)* Chair…

FIRST R'MAN: *(Careering in.)* MY GIRL

SECOND R'MAN: *(Enraged.)* Wash you said

FIRST R'MAN: MY GIRL

LAZAR: Shh

SECOND R'MAN: Not washing is he

LAZAR: Shh

SECOND R'MAN: Not washing at all

LAZAR: *(Thundering.)* SHUT UP IT'S A RESURRECTION

(The RIVERMEN stop, and peer at the scene. SISI's gentle laugh comes from the handcart. As LAZAR lowers himself into his chair, the man closes his umbrella and sings, mournfully and religiously. SISI's knees lift, her legs enclose TAX and at last fall again. The river flows…as the man is about to depart, TAX calls out to him.)

TAX: Christ had a dog…

(The MAN stops.)

How many people know that?

(TAX climbs off SISI's body.)
It wasn't that he wanted the dog the dog
followed him

MAN: Yes

TAX: *(Puzzled.)* You knew that you knew Christ had a
dog?

MAN: Yes

(TAX is thoughtful…)

TAX: You knew that you knew that even though it is
not mentioned in the Scriptures?

MAN: What need was there to mention it it's obvious

TAX: Is it?

MAN: All that is obvious is unmentioned that is the
mark of a great book surely?

TAX: Yes
Yes

(The MAN is about to go.)
Presumably it was a thoroughbred?
(The MAN stops again.)
A thoroughbred and not a crossbreed not a
mongrel?

MAN: A thoroughbred

TAX: *(Nodding his agreement.)* Yes yes
(He smiles broadly.)
I was about to ask how you could be certain but
I feel sure you will say

MAN: It's obvious

TAX: Yes
(TAX smiles.)
Yes
I knew you would say that

MAN: *(Returning a few paces.)* Obvious for this reason
that Christ surrounded himself with outcasts
sinners and the unfortunate wealth and
distinction nauseated him
(Pause. TAX strains to comprehend.)

TAX: Yes
(He grapples.)

Yes

So

(His hand writhes in the air.)

So

(He shakes his head in frustration.)

So the dog

(He stops, fathoming.)

The dog should have been a stray surely an
outcast mangey and a mongrel?

(The MAN is still.)

I don't understand if everything is obvious why
it isn't obvious the dog should have been

(He stops. The MAN simply looks…)

You mean

(His hands describe his effort.)

You must mean

(His eyes meet the MAN's eyes… the MAN withdraws.)

The dog frustrated him?

Yes

Yes

Precisely because Christ had this preference for
strays criminals and vagrants this dog would
have to be elegant expensive and coiffured

(He shakes his head.)

That is what you mean by obvious you mean
it's obvious this dog was all that Christ abhorred
yes the dog was sent to try him as all life tried
him no wonder the disciples threw stones at it a
thoroughbred yes it had belonged originally to a
wealthy woman

(He is delighted with his reasoning.)

It's obvious

(He grins.)

The dog saw Christ and ran after him she called
she whistled she stamped her foot so what the
animal was incurably mischievous…

*(TAX realizes the RIVERMEN are staring at him with
profound hostility. He falls silent for a moment…)*

Never Christ without a dog never virtue without
mockery…

*

6

BUDA prunes geraniums.

LAZAR: I thought she was a suicide I thought she could
not live without me I was mistaken Bubo
strangled her
(Pause. The secateurs…)
Thinking her a suicide I was not deeply troubled
the bend is not without its charm and after all I
took it as a compliment to me now all I think of
is the loss the loss and the futility Bubo carried
her in his arms down three boulevards and in
broad daylight no one took the slightest notice
Sisi looked good in a man's arms I want him
hanged this passion to hang Bubo has wrung
more life from me sorry I had to speak to
someone my son is mad do you mind if I
(Pause. The secateurs.)
You don't offer me a chair if any man needed
a chair it's me but you don't offer such things
are not lost on me as for coffee I can smell it
the smell is oh the smell of coffee on a sunlit
morning but it's not on offer evidently neither
coffee nor a chair
(Pause. The secateurs.)

BUDA: If I offer you a chair you'll sit in it
(Pause.)

LAZAR: Yes and if you offer coffee

BUDA: You will drink it Lazar I am a widow how great
is our satisfaction only widows know the fact you
are not dead yet is

LAZAR: A detail

BUDA:	Yes
LAZAR:	And my dying has been in any case
BUDA:	Interminable
LAZAR:	Yes it is in many ways a pity I did not perish in the field altogether a pity Bubo did not murder me he might have done a casual fist a kick in passing you know Bubo
BUDA:	It's your face
LAZAR:	Yes
BUDA:	Please go now Lazar I am so happy here please go
LAZAR:	Yes

(He bites his lip, reluctant to leave…)
Lazar had a wife…
(He chews his tongue.)
He had a wife and he thought in his crisis he would carry his pain to his wife and she being a wife would bear some of it rather as if the pain being a heavy bag she took one handle and they staggered on like refugees through some awesome railway station and if she fell he lifted her and if he fell it was her that lifted him is that sentimental it is it is sentimental Lazar was his own best critic one day I was rich not only rich but glamorous and when I ceased to be rich still I was glamorous then suddenly I was old and neither rich nor glamorous too bad too late too everything…
(Pause. BUDA shakes her head with weary contempt. She seems about to speak but abandons it.)
Preposterous…

BUDA:	Yes
LAZAR:	Buda was she not also glamorous?
BUDA:	Buda was…

(She declines his invitation to recriminate.)

LAZAR:	A quarrel would have been nice
BUDA:	Would it?
LAZAR:	In some ways yes there is life in a quarrel

BUDA: *(Shaking her head.)* No chair no coffee and no
quarrelling
(LAZAR seems shaken, then pulls himself together.)

LAZAR: I kill Bubo

BUDA: Yes

LAZAR: Oh yes I find Bubo and I kill him

BUDA: Yes
(LAZAR takes a determined step, and stops.)

LAZAR: And if they kill me for killing him

BUDA: So what?

LAZAR: So what?

BUDA: You are dying anyway
*(They look at one another. BUDA struggles. She clings
to her resolution.)*
We must move on we must we must
*(LAZAR leaves. BUDA is still. She slowly dissolves
in tears. The naked figure of JANUARY appears. He
consoles her.)*

*

7

*A café. Seated at a table LAZAR and BUBO. After a long silence, they
burst out laughing. The silence returns, for the same duration. They
burst out laughing again, and cease again. CANAL enters, exquisite.
BUBO and LAZAR rise, an exhibition of formality. LAZAR goes to kiss
CANAL's extended hand.*

LAZAR: My head is not my own
(He and BUBO laugh identically and stop.)
It's not
It's not my own the things that just walk in walk
in and take up residence trains laundries flocks
of birds and last night yes an entire orchestra
(He and BUBO laugh again.)
I turned the light on and then I turned it off I
smacked my ears I hummed I coughed this is

232

Bubo did I mention him age is an estate but all
the gates have fallen in come the scum the scum
the scum drive in no walls no privacy nothing
(He stares at CANAL.)
POLICE
POLICE
(They all laugh now.)
They always were a rumour Bubo says Bubo
knows
(Pause, then they all sit.)
Bubo's on the run I say on the run quaint phrase
on the run from whom from what Bubo has
never once been interviewed have you Bubo
even once been interviewed and he is the
murderer he makes no secret of it do you Bubo
both the murderer and the chief suspect so what
does it follow he is entitled to be interviewed
who does Bubo think he is hanging around here
drawing attention to himself POLICE POLICE
(LAZAR and BUBO laugh again.)
What's more
(They laugh uncontrollably.)
What's more
HE FEELS GUILTY YES HE EXPERIENCES
REMORSE
*(BUBO is quiet. In the pause, LAZAR moves his spoon
idly in the saucer…)*
Of course Bubo is a peasant killing comes
naturally to him
(He lifts his eyes to BUBO.)
It comes naturally to me THERE IT IS AGAIN
(He shakes his head.)
Bells now
(He thrusts his finger in his ear.)
Bells not Stefansdom more local pretty in some
ways a wedding no not even that a baker's shop
on top of steam engines of course on top of gas

leaks such a busy head such a such a busy head
and yet
(He smiles oddly at CANAL.)
It's as if to spare me the fatigue of travelling the
globe the globe has moved into my head Africa
next hyenas the Nile cataracts whole landscapes
workshops school playgrounds such a busy head
and yet
(Pause.)
A single woman entering a single woman
dressed how shall we say a single woman
dressed as you are dressed
(Pause.)
Commands silence where should I be without
her I should have died in infancy not really
silence I mean I cease to hear it
(Pause.)
Bubo is a peasant but as he says all men were
peasants once lords even and I acknowledge this
don't I Bubo I have heard lords making love
lords and poets clerics actors men of impeccable
impeccable impeccable what
(He smiles.)
culture impeccable culture and I must say once
they were on the mattress the peasant rose up
they shut their eyes they pumped they thrust
they laughed they cursed they slapped they
shoved poor cursing poor slapping because one
has to state there is even in cursing a measure
of refinement the women were the same I don't
discriminate
*(He stands. He seems to suffer an attack. CANAL rises
to support him.)*

CANAL: Never you
           Never you
           (He shakes his head.)
           And never us

(Embarrassed, BUBO coughs slightly and withdraws.
LAZAR recovers. He sits. He wipes his eyes…)
He's leaving

LAZAR: Yes

CANAL: *(Alarmed.)* He's going out

LAZAR: My sentimentality it's too much for him

CANAL: LAZAR HE'S GOING OUT

LAZAR: It's too much for everybody

CANAL: LAZAR

LAZAR: *(Coolly.)* He'll be back
(CANAL sits.)
He needs me the murderer of my wife he needs
me have you seen his eyes dog's eyes I don't
dislike dogs we had forty on the estate shepherds
hunters terriers my son says I am one but can a
dog have a dog it's a conundrum
(He looks intently at CANAL…a thin wind blows.
Suddenly LAZAR rises, toppling his chair)
I NEED TO STAND
I NEED TO STAND
(His body aches. Flurries of snow…)

*

8

A waste. Snow and wind. Distant dogs.
Rusting medical trolleys drift and collide. At last a filthy surgeon
enters, pulling off his gloves.

SMAJE: I didn't try sometimes you don't feel like it
one procedure follows on another I could see I
would be here until midnight and my knee hurts
sorry Mr Mr I never know their names sorry
if you were a woman it would have been the
same only a girl only a beautiful girl or an infant
possibly might have made me scrupulous sorry
(He notices LAZAR.)

| | Are you a relative they die these boys because God wants them to neither you nor I can impose ourselves between them and their destiny pity even seems superfluous and today I had a headache a headache and a painful knee |

LAZAR: See a doctor

SMAJE: I should do when I speak of God I hardly know what I am saying but still I must say God I must say it I don't trust doctors

LAZAR: No

SMAJE: I'd rather have the knee

LAZAR: Same with me and my brain they tell me its routine the surgery but

SMAJE: Routine yes but the surgeon might be married the marriage might be under strain

LAZAR: The very morning of the operation

SMAJE: The wife admits her infidelity

LAZAR: Precisely all the same it's noisy and
(*A trolley drifts in.*)
getting noisier
(*LAZAR stares as the trolley comes to a stop. The body of TAX lies on it, naked…*)
It's me who's
(*He swallows.*)
It's me who's meant to be
(*He writhes.*)
I'M THE ONE WHO'S DYING I LAZAR I
(*He takes a kick at the trolley but it nearly topples him.*)
Ow
Ow
I loved you little boy oh little little boy I
Ow
(*He nurses his knee. He weeps.*)
I bought him Tacitus I bought him Plutarch we walked to school reciting the
(*He stops. He shakes his head.*)
Not every day

Not every day
(He shrugs.)
Rarely his mother was a suicide he lived with
me he
(He shakes his head.)
I never went to school with him not once he had
a nurse she
(He falls silent… at last he lifts his eyes.)
Christ had a dog he said
(He frowns.)
I never went to school with him not once in
seven years the nurse I stripped her as she came
back through the door stripped her laid her on
the floor that was school school meant a naked
nurse to me
(He gulps…)

SMAJE: It's true

LAZAR: Oh little boy oh little little boy does suicide run
in families his mother she was a suicide did I say
she drowned herself I did say I did say

SMAJE: It's true Christ had a dog he beat the dog this
had no effect still the dog loved him in the end
he killed the dog few people know this even
fewer now why kill the dog because the dog was
love he didn't crucify it so far as we know you
cannot crucify a dog its anatomy the disposition
of the limbs hanging however dogs have been
hanged…

LAZAR: *(Moving away from the body, fingers in ears.)* A new
noise now…
(He peers at the ground. He shakes his head.)
A cardboard box…
(He jerks his head.)
A giant ripping a cardboard box you see I come
back to myself a dead child but I come back to
myself dead boy dead wife but still I
(He shudders.)
no not a box a train AND IT WHISTLES IT
WHISTLES forty carriages restaurant sleeping

cars only the best trains for Lazar blue the livery
all blue…
(He lifts his eyes to SMAJE…)
I'm dying but dying is a queue and they jump in
they shove in front of me
(He shrugs. BUBO enters with LAZAR's chair.)
DON'T DIE YOU
(BUBO looks puzzled.)
He will of course you see he will the moment I
loved Bubo I knew he would be taken from me
isn't that right Bubo?
(BUBO shrugs. He unfolds the chair…)
Sit in it yourself
*(BUBO hesitates, then obeys LAZAR. LAZAR pushes out
the trolley on which TAX lies.)*

SMAJE: I didn't try
(He lifts his hands, pitifully.)
I didn't try
(He bites his lip.)
Some days you don't feel like it
(A cold wind blows over BUBO…)

*

9

BUBO alone.

BUBO: Killer he says killer
(Pause.)
I don't like that I was a farmer I say you *were* a
farmer he says *were* a farmer *were*
(Pause.)
I killed I say does that make me a killer he says
you might have been a poet you might have
been a nurse now you are a killer the killer kills
the poet the killer kills the nurse
(Pause.)

So kill he says kill Lazar
(He leaps off the chair.)
I DON'T HAVE THE INCLINATION
I SAY WHO CARES ABOUT YOUR
INCLINATION HE SAYS DO IT ANYWAY I
LIKE YOU I SAY YOU LIKED SISI HE SAYS
IN BED I SAY IN BED I DIDN'T MEAN TO
DO IT BUT SHE SAID
(Pause.)
She said
(He stops. He shudders…)
A woman must be careful what she says in bed
(He sits again.)
He calls it arithmetic
(Pause.)
Killing he calls arithmetic how's that I say
because if you kill both of us you'll get away but
if you kill one only you will hang I'm going to
the magistrate today stop me Bubo slit my throat
and smash my head never I say never will I hurt
that head it's full of noise he says help Lazar find
some silence
*(BUBO shakes his head bitterly. He is on the verge of
tears but then stands up, reluctant but determined. He
takes a length of rope from the back of the chair and
flings it high over a beam. He makes a noose, then
climbs on the chair adjusting the length and tension.
LAZAR enters stiffly…)*

LAZAR:	I looked at the lake
BUBO:	No good?
LAZAR:	So cold the lake
BUBO:	All right but the railway?
LAZAR:	Ugly
BUBO:	Ugly yes but
LAZAR:	Think of the driver
BUBO:	The driver?
LAZAR:	The driver yes the moment he applies the brake how terrible it is that perfectly redundant act of

pity an instinct possibly an instinct not to hurt
another even when the other is unknown to him
where does it come from Bubo in that instant
this humble engine driver becomes superior to
Christ to Christ's whole teaching superior no I
prefer not to be the subject of an impulse I have
always scrupulously denied myself you must do
it Bubo with the rope...
*(BUBO shrugs, unwilling to act... he climbs off the
chair. He looks at LAZAR...)*

BUBO: I want to say a few things do you mind a few
things obviously nothing I say will be well said
what am I after all a killer a killer who was a
farmer a farmer who sold everything to buy
a girl a bed leaving his children destitute a
heartless brutal and degenerate character who

LAZAR: *(Going to the chair.)* I'll sit if you don't mind

BUBO: Who then destroyed the only thing he ever
loved in a fit of temper a pig a horse a great-
fisted lout a humourless baboon but

LAZAR: *(Jumping up, a finger to his ear.)* A CHOIR NOW

BUBO: Then he met his master and the master said I
forgive you

LAZAR: A CHOIR SINGING PSALMS

BUBO: Forgive me I said how can I be forgiven when
by the riverside a young girl adored by you is
lying dead?

LAZAR: THE PSALMS AND THE BELLS
TOGETHER
(He shakes his head.)
INTOLERABLE HELP ME UP HELP ME UP
BUBO
(He extends a hand.)

BUBO: I just

LAZAR: I know I know

BUBO: Just want to say

LAZAR: I know what you want to say

BUBO: YOU DON'T YOU DON'T KNOW WHAT I
WANT TO SAY

LAZAR: I DID NOT FORGIVE YOU AND SISI WAS
NO GIRL
(He stares at BUBO… Pause)
Sisi was forty and what I said was
(He lifts a hand limply.)
It doesn't matter what I said
*(He tries to mount the chair but is stuck with one foot
up and one down. He thrusts a hand at BUBO…)*

BUBO: *(Denying him.)* My speech…
(LAZAR is exasperated, disbelieving.)
Let a poor man make a speech
(Pause. LAZAR tries to extricate himself but fails.)

LAZAR: Bubo you are the executioner at executions it is
customary for the victim to make a speech

BUBO: THE EXECUTIONER WILL MAKE A
SPEECH
(Pause. LAZAR glares. BUBO is unrelenting.)

LAZAR: SPEAK THEN SPEAK I CAN'T HEAR IT
ANYWAY
(BUBO waits for a moment, preparing himself.)

BUBO: Forgive me I said how can I be forgiven I am
unforgivable and the master said
*(He shakes his head with the pleasure of the
recollection.)*
the master said I shall never forget the mild
expression on his face a remarkable face full of
pain but pain dug-in a field his face I thought the
master's face is a field in Autumn when we dig
in the stubble of the crops so his pain was lying
in the furrows a thin crust on top he said I killed
oh killer I killed in my heart every woman I
have loved…
(BUBO shakes his head sadly.)

LAZAR: Did I say that?
(BUBO nods.)

	Under certain conditions even Lazar was conventional
BUBO:	DON'T SPOIL IT
LAZAR:	It is conventional Bubo
BUBO:	*(Wounded.)* Shut up
LAZAR:	So thoroughly conventional that even the cynical calculation that such banal sentiments would serve to comfort you cannot excuse my uttering them
BUBO:	Shut up Shut up
LAZAR:	HANG ME THEN HANG ME *(BUBO frowns…)* When Lazar spoke trash he forfeited his right to further life HANG HIM HANG HIM FOR HIS SPIRITUAL POVERTY *(BUBO shrugs.)*
BUBO:	Trash was it let it be trash and let me be a pig since trash pleases me IT WAS A LOVELY THING TO SAY I SAY LOVELY *(A pause… then wind blows over them… with a sudden rush BUBO goes to heave LAZAR onto the chair but cannot lift him. LAZAR lets out a cry of pain.)* I HATE YOU I HATE YOU
LAZAR:	HANG ME THEN *(BUBO's desperate attempts to hoist LAZAR onto the chair fail. LAZAR topples and falls with a cry into the snow. He lies still. BUBO wails and sobs in the wind. The rope floats in the air…)*
BUBO:	I'm going home *(A pause, then he laughs hysterically and stops.)* I have no home *(He laughs again and stops…)* SO WHAT I'M GOING THERE

(He pulls his coat tightly round himself and sets off with determination. After a few paces he stops. He chooses another direction instead. He marches off. Suddenly he collapses and dies without a sound…)

LAZAR: Bubo…

(Pause. LAZAR contrives to roll onto his back.)

Bubo…

(He lifts himself onto his elbows…)

Death's a woman Bubo I've just realised this all these images of old men with scythes and hourglasses no she's young young and got her skirts up she's a whore a young whore Bubo bare-arsed no underwear a young whore but a whore who cannot be seduced not by me anyway AN UNSEDUCIBLE WHORE solve that conundrum Bubo

(Pause.)

Lazar was a seducer always always he seduced years after desire years after love the rotted language the rotted looks and still they flung their clothes off not this time however IN MY OWN TIME SAYS THE BARE-ARSED WHORE IN MY OWN TIME

(He scoffs.)

Lazar recoiled he was not accustomed to the mockery of women…

(Pause.)

Help me up…

(He extends a hand…)

*

10

A table. An exquisite white cloth. Gleaming silverware.
A party of guests sweeps in, voluble, a cacophony of pleasantries and
debates. This endures…
LAZAR is delivered to them. They are suddenly silent.

LAZAR: I want to suck your fuckhole I want to suck I
            want to suck
            (They are neither shocked nor amused…a single drink
            is poured…)
            I want to suck your fuckhole I want to suck I
            want to suck
            (The stillness is slowly eroded. A murmured
            conversation… LAZAR stares into space.)
            I want to suck your fuckhole I want to suck I
            (The party becomes animated again…)
            want to suck
            (LAZAR is obscured as the guests move to and fro, the
            cacophony rising. He is obliged to raise his voice…)
            I want to suck your fuckhole I want to
            (He is stopped as a guest empties a glass over his head.
            Laughter and derision…)
            suck I
            (And further reactions…)
            want to suck I
            (A second glass is emptied over LAZAR. He is silenced,
            but only briefly…)
            I want to suck your fuckhole I want to suck I
            want to suck
            (The persistence of LAZAR and the jeering that
            accompanies it cease to amuse. One of the guests,
            adopting a clinical attitude, perches on a reversed chair
            and studies him, chin in hand…)
            I want to suck your fuckhole I want to suck I
            want to suck
            (Others follow suit, leaning on the back of chairs or
            placing their arms round the shoulders of their wives.

*Just as LAZAR resembles a parrot in his manner, so
they adopt the attitudes of zoo-visitors…)*
I want to suck your fuckhole I want to suck I
want to suck I want to suck your fuckhole I want
to
*(For no apparent reason LAZAR stops. The guests wait
patiently…he declines to satisfy them…)*

GUEST: Suck…?
              *(Laughter…he is adamantly silent…at last some
              desultory conversation starts up, unrelated to LAZAR.)*

LAZAR: Suck I want to suck I want to suck your fuckhole
              I want to suck I want to suck
              *(Even the curious are now fatigued. The party recovers
              its momentum. LAZAR is irregular in his recital
              and ignored…the hum of the party returns…guests
              manoeuvre…one individual sits by LAZAR with a
              glass, unaware of the decay of the party, the failing
              light, the diminishing number of guests…)*

TAWPAW: Christ had a dog…
              *(Pause. A coarse laugh comes from the shadowed
              room…)*
              Not everybody knows this obviously the dog
              was vital to him an irritation certainly but often
              what is irritable is necessary…
              (Two party guests are flirting in the shadows.)
              For if we take it as axiomatic that all Christ
              taught was perfect its perfection nevertheless
              required the contrast of the imperfect to be
              understood just as an alabaster statue shows
              better on a dark ground or black pencil is more
              vivid on white paper
              (He shrugs.)
              My metaphors aren't very good…!
              *(From the shadow, the murmuring of seduction. A
              glass breaks. The lovers laugh.)*
              And this dog we can say without fear of
              contradiction had the characteristics of all dogs
              for example

(The woman of the pair emits a little cry as the man lowers her over the white clothed table.)
It was entirely instinctual it was uninhibited by all considerations of good or bad outcomes it was after all
(Her skirt is drawn back.)
a dog…!
(She moans…)
And Christ saw this always always he saw the life of the dog for he saw everything it goes without saying
(She gasps…)
He saw and
(She cries again…)
disapproved but *whilst* disapproving – and this is the paradox embedded in his teaching – Christ simultaneously recognized the absolute necessity of its depravity even to this extent that hanging on the cross he endured the spectacle of
(The lovers laugh intimately…)
his own dog copulating with a bitch or even several and
WAS
NOT
MOCKED…
(TAWPAW shakes his head over his own meditation. LAZAR is still for some time…)

LAZAR: *(Defiantly.)* I want to suck your fuckhole I want to suck I want to suck
(They stare cruelly at one another…)
I want to suck your fuckhole I want to suck I want to suck
(TAWPAW abandons LAZAR with a gesture of contempt. He draws the male lover into another room with a cruel laugh. The woman remains on the table, gazing at LAZAR. He stares at her, uncompromising, charmless. Opening her thighs, she lies along the table, her head tilted back, so her face is invisible to him…)

NANA: I show I show how hard it is to show I show
myself to an old man hard because he is not old
I know his infancy his terrible infancy the child
went to women he knew nothing of women
asking them asking and stammering asking and
blushing asking what was under their clothes
and they showed him and he looked he looked
at what lay under their clothes so deep was
his look it scoured their bellies it scalded their
thighs and they squirmed and they shifted they
were scared of his eyes and they shouted now
you must touch all men touch as soon as they've
looked but he only looked so they dragged
down their clothes they were bruised and
bewildered so deep was this look they felt more
than naked they felt stripped to the bone and
they smacked him they raged and they smacked
for every look there must be an act do the act
do the act but still he refrained he did not save
them from themselves with his act I'm the same
I'm the same
*(She jerks upright, swinging her legs off the table and
tightening her skirt over her knees.)*
The looking the searching I'm the same
(She slides off the table.)
NO WOMAN LIKES A MAN WHO LIKES
WOMEN SO MUCH
(She flings out of the room.)

LAZAR: I didn't hear that
I'm deaf
I DIDN'T HEAR THAT
*(LAZAR tries to rise off his chair. He staggers and
clutches at the table. The cloth comes with him as he
falls in a cascade of silver and glass. He lies still in the
dim light…)*
They show
(He shifts a little.)
They show

(A leg rises and falls.)
THEY SHOW THEY SHOW AND STILL
YOU CANNOT KNOW YOU GO TO
ANOTHER OH LAZAR'S FIFTEEN
HUNDRED VISITS TO THE MOUTH OF
GOD AM I NOT THE TRUE SERVANT OF
THE FAITH I CRAVE ENTRANCE I CRAVE
AND PSALM-SINGING AND PRAYER-
CHANTING YES LAZAR GREW HARD
KNEES FROM STOOPING NOT ONLY TO
THE CITY'S CUNT BUT TO THE CUNT OF
THE WILDERNESS
(Pause.)
And cunt was sometimes pleased and sometimes
turned black looks on him for that is the way of
God that is the sign of Him
(He pulls himself up.)
A little silver travelled from her dark his stuff
his unloved stuff I watched the creeping stream
like chained prisoners emerging from some deep
incarceration or an army crawling from defeat
but did she reach between her legs to take it on
her fingers did she bless her lips with it no she
did not it was muck to her it was ANOTHER
SNOT
(He scoffs.)
And her thick flood of ecstasy did he describe
it as the tide of Heaven did he inhale it did he
anoint his head with it never BUT CURSED
THE STAINING OF HIS TROUSERS
(He scoffs. He staggers, he grasps the table.)
No
No
There was Christ and there was Lazar two only
ONLY TWO and what they loved the few who
knew them understood only dimly
(He senses another in the room.)
Dimly don't you think?

*(LAZAR looks to see BUDA, motionless and entirely
clad in mourning, revealed in the obscurity. She is
mouthing a prayer but no sound comes from her lips.
LAZAR protests.)*

CAN'T HEAR YOU CAN'T HEAR IT CAN'T
HEAR YOU

(She seems unaware of him.)

Niagara

Thirty steel works all on overtime

Steel works with buglers on the chimney tops

Forty buglers insane every one

Dustcarts falling over cliffs

Horse dancing on a drum

(She prays.)

CAN'T HEAR YOU CAN'T HEAR IT CAN'T
HEAR YOU

*(BUDA emits a long howl of grief. LAZAR hears her
now, and covers his ears. The sound he has listed
fills the room as he implores her to notice him…
the cacophony ceases suddenly as CANAL runs in, in
mourning and pulling a black coat round herself.)*

CANAL: Are we late

Are we late

Yes we're late YOU SCUM YOU FILTH YOU
SCUM

*(She turns on JANUARY, who saunters idly in her
footsteps…)*

We're late

(He stops. He shrugs.)

JANUARY: Sorry

CANAL: *(To BUDA.)* He started he saw me and he started I
couldn't

BUDA: It's all right

CANAL: Get him off and once he started I started

BUDA: Obviously

CANAL: THE OX

BUDA: It's all right

CANAL: THE OX-BRAINED OX-ARSED

249

BUDA:	It's all right
CANAL:	OX
	(JANUARY hangs his head…)
	I drove so fast I nearly killed someone
	IMAGINE IF I'D KILLED SOMEONE
	(She threatens JANUARY, who shakes his head like a schoolboy… her rage softens… her hand travels to her mouth… she giggles… she cannot stifle her giggling…)
BUDA:	I said I am happily married thank you he said I dispute this thesis
CANAL:	A CHILD OR SOMETHING
BUDA:	It is not a thesis I said it is a simple statement of the truth
CANAL:	A DEAD CHILD ALL BECAUSE
BUDA:	He said that is itself wreathed in contradiction
CANAL:	A DEAD CHILD FOR YOUR
BUDA:	WREATHED IN CONTRADICTION HOW VERY LAZAR I WAS TO HEAR THAT OFTEN IN THE COMING YEARS
CANAL:	LITTLE
BUDA:	WREATHED IN CONTRADICTION
CANAL:	LITTLE
	(She stops giggling…)
BUDA:	I was however I was happily married

*

LEARNING KNEELING

Characters

STURDEE
A Legless Landlord

OLIM
A Lifelong Mistress

FLANGE
A Gardener

DOUGHTY
A Dancing Adolescent

COADE
A Dancing Adolescent

LUX
A Bride

DEMONSTRATOR
An Incursion

SONG
Assistant to Demonstrator

I

A vast absence, of a culture and its artefacts. A seated man, torpid, a relic. A youth runs in, seething and pale.

FLANGE: They're coming / what are we doing? / anything? /
(The relic is still.)
Anything or nothing? /
(And remains so.)
They're coming / and we're doing nothing? /
(Flange decays.)
We're doing nothing then? / nothing at all? /
(Flange recedes. Silence returns. An old woman enters, supported on a cane.)

OLIM: They're coming /
(She passes over the stage.)
We're not doing anything / are we? / what is there to do? /
(She goes out. Silence returns.)

STURDEE: In the long run / and the long run is / I am the first to admit it / a dubious category / uncharitable in its verdicts / withering in its objectivity / for all that / a necessary counter to the short run / clumsy and fetid as the short run tends to be / in the long run / what good did it do us? /
(Two adolescent girls enter, peculiarly attired and holding hands. They indicate. They flutter. They bite their lips.)
They're coming / yes / they're coming but it's Wednesday /

OLIM: *(Passing back over the stage.)* We're doing nothing / for the perfectly good reason / that there is nothing to do / I appreciate that is too logical for some people /
(She goes out.)

STURDEE: It did us no good at all / what it did do /
however / was to obliterate any possibility / of
doing anything else / anything else / necessarily
including things both worse and better than the
thing we did do / stand in the light you two / the
light is cruel / the shade might make you / as all
dark does /
(He shakes his head with contempt.)
Enticing /
*(The girls edge into the light. STURDEE contemplates
them.)*
Oh / the utter poverty / the barren / paltry /
rudiments of gender in you / do something /

DOUGHTY/CODE: *(Apprehensively.)* They're coming /

STURDEE: They're coming / it's true / but we insist on
doing what we do best / in my case / thinking
/ in yours / dancing / dancing badly / so badly
you cause me to think in ways I would not think
if you danced better / now / is that so strange to
you? / dance / dance badly /
*(The girls, not only from the effect of their terror,
perform a parody of ballet. STURDEE watches. In the
vast space, the sound of their clumsy feet. They falter.)*
Badly / badly dance /
*(Frowning and humiliated the girls skip, twirl and
trip under STURDEE's gaze.)*
Oh / how perfectly you rebuke not only me /
but the entire theology of love / its sculpture /
its poetry / I am nauseated / nauseated but not
sufficiently / dance worse / dance worse /
*(The girls exert themselves to satisfy STURDEE, who
shakes his head in contempt.)*
The hyperbole of desire / how thoroughly
you extirpate it beneath your stamping feet /
DANCE WORSE /
(The girls are an apotheosis of the grotesque.)
How I love Wednesday / Wednesday is beautiful
to me /

OLIM: *(Entering.)* Let them go now /

STURDEE: Yes / they can go /
(OLIM claps her hands. DOUGHTY and COADE cease their antics, breathless, perspiring and resentful.)
See you next week /
(The girls go to leave.)
If there is a next week /
(They look appalled.)
They're coming / aren't they? / you said so yourself / many things may happen / or rather few / we know nothing /

OLIM: We know nothing / so until we do / should we not assume the unfaltering repetition of the routine we have become accustomed to? / there seems to me no obvious advantage in adopting any other course /

STURDEE: Wednesday it is / then /
(DOUGHTY and COADE go to leave.)
Thank you for your ugliness / your clumsiness / your charmlessness / etcetera / possibly because *they* are coming / some further weight of dread was added to your usual ponderous performance / you surpassed yourselves /
(They scowl and depart. The room fills with silence as water fills a jar. OLIM regards STURDEE with a detachment practised and enjoyed.)

OLIM: Let them come / let them come I say / if it puts a stop to this /

STURDEE: A stop to what? /
(She denies him.)
To what might their coming put a stop to? /

OLIM: THIS / THIS /
(Now he regards her.)

STURDEE: As ever / so ruthless / so withering of subtlety / nuance / or sensibility / is your self-consciousness / you assume the subject of your preoccupations must simultaneously be the preoccupation of everybody else / THIS

/ is meaningless to me / THIS / THIS / twice
meaningless /
(They hang on stares.)

OLIM: Never will I be forgiven / never / will I? / never
forgiven my decay /

STURDEE: Never / no /

OLIM: And yours / your worse decay / lends you no
pity / for mine / that's why I say / let them come
/
(STURDEE contrives a smile.)

STURDEE: You hope they will hurt me / I promise you
/ if I'm not shot in the first splash of anger / I
will not be / ever / ever / shot / furthermore
/ I expect / in a rather short time / to gain an
imperishable ascendancy over them / but I
sound complacent /

OLIM: *(Alerted.)* TRUCKS / LISTEN / TRUCKS /

STURDEE: Trucks / yes / but whereas it might be their
trucks coming / equally / it might be ours
driving away / noise is a liar on a day like this /
where are you going? /

OLIM: *(Apprehensive.)* I'm lying down /

STURDEE: Unwise /

OLIM: I have a headache /

STURDEE: When did you not have a headache? /

OLIM: This is worse and in a different place / I am
lying on the bed /

STURDEE: *(To arrest her.)* UNWISE / I SAID /
(She stops.)

OLIM: Sturdee / I am old / and ill / and ugly /

STURDEE: You are / you are all those things / and yet / still
female / horizontal / and on a bed /

OLIM: YOU KNOW NOTHING /
(She walks away, but stops, leaning on her cane.)
How right if I / a loyal wife / stood by her
husband's chair / proud the pair of us / and
slaughtered / bled together / bleeding but not

caring any more for draining blood or going life
/ dead on the same floor / right / entirely right /
(Her voice cracks.)
Never / never however /
*(She seethes. STURDEE lifts one hand off the arm
of his chair, and lets it fall, a concession to the facts.
OLIM seems to sway, then goes out. At once, FLANGE
hurtles in, with an armful of weapons.)*

FLANGE: It is them / it is them / do you want a shotgun? /
do you want a knife? /

STURDEE: Do I want a shotgun? / no / I don't think I want
a shotgun /

FLANGE: All right / have a knife /
*(In organizing his armoury, FLANGE spills the entire
collection over the floor.)*
FUCK / FUCK /
*(He kneels. He grabs a knife and extends it to
STURDEE.)*

STURDEE: I think / probably / no knife /
(FLANGE is desolated.)

FLANGE: No knife? / but you could kill one of them / as
he leaned over you / in the stomach / jab once /
jab twice /

STURDEE: Probably / probably I could /
(Their eyes meet cruelly.)
Still / no knife /
(FLANGE lets the knife throb between his fingers.)

FLANGE: You are old / and sick / and fixed in a chair /
what is it worth / your life? /

STURDEE: That question I have asked myself / when I was
neither old / nor sick / nor in a chair / when I
was wringing wet from women / gushing girls
/ and seething wives / I asked it when I was
adolescent / and when I was a child / half-way
in a game / or stiff with horror in the night / and
I got no answer / why? / because value cannot
be attached to life / life is / life does / keep your
weights and measures for the greengrocer / so

now go and fight / what are you? / a gardener /
they will wipe you off the world / and you have
not trimmed the box / pity /

FLANGE: Fuck the box /

STURDEE: Fuck it / indeed /

FLANGE: I don't make hedges for the enemy to drape
their laundry on /

STURDEE: Flange / you are inspired / don't let me delay
your imminent epiphany /
*(FLANGE gathers up his armoury. He stops at the
door.)*

FLANGE: If I see them with you / and you are smiling /
Mr Sturdee / your head comes off / heed my
warning /

STURDEE: There are smiles / and smiles / Flange / some
lavish / some strained through a sieve of
expediency /

FLANGE: That is a fine distinction / I doubt / will carry
weight with me /
(He goes to leave. Some thought delays him.)
I never / in all our years /

STURDEE: All our years? / you are descending into
sentimentality / it can't have been more than
three /
*(FLANGE's injured look injures STURDEE in turn.
STURDEE looks to the floor.)*

FLANGE: In the three years / Miss Olim and you /
employed me / I never felt anything but
gratitude to you / and when people said / aren't
they peculiar / those two / they shout and cry
like children / I said yes / but you don't know
their history / do you? / no more do I / so I
don't criticize /

STURDEE: *(Without sarcasm.)* That is typically kind of you /
and if you were grateful / Flange / Olim and I /
we were grateful too /
(FLANGE bites his lip. He turns to go.)

FLANGE / THEY WILL DISARM YOU /
AND STICK YOUR PEN-KNIVES IN YOUR
EYES /
(FLANGE seems to falter, but only momentarily.)

FLANGE: Probably / probably they will do /
(He will not look at STURDEE.)
I love this garden / as much / and maybe more
than you / I stop sometimes / or rather / I don't
stop / it stops me / the wet lawns / the scents
/ the climbers on the walls / what Miss Olim
does / it's poetry / but outside the walls / the
hatred / you know the hatred / Mr Sturdee /
and the more it stinks / this hate / the more we
look the other way / plant this / plant that / as if
honeysuckle could keep killers away /
(He frowns.)
I'm saying /
(His mouth moves wordlessly.)
I'm saying /
(He struggles.)
WHAT IS A GARDEN / MR STURDEE /
IT'S CIVILITY /
(He raises his eyes to STURDEE.)
And there is none / so /
(He breathes with difficulty.)
Let it go now / let it run to seed /
*(STURDEE senses the rebuke in FLANGE's words and
resumes his solidity. FLANGE seems to hang on the air,
then he turns away energetically. An oppressive silence
descends, swiftly relieved by an urgent whispering
and the hissing of stiff gowns sweeping the floor. A
bride emerges from the obscurity, her infant attendants
supporting her train. She marches to STURDEE and
stops before him. She bursts into tears.)*

STURDEE: *(As she recovers.)* Filthy is the bride / organza
notwithstanding / filthy / or is it taffeta / silk
taffeta? / these fabrics / even the names /
hyperbole / the filthier the bride the more

263

submerged she is in bolts of stuff / Thirty metres
/ fifty possibly / blinding white / can't look
/ dark glasses / someone / please / and the
perfume / this is / oh / certainly this is virginity
/ I'd like to kiss your arse / but they are here
/ by the truckload evidently / or was the truck
your cortège / stuck here / you see nothing /
(The bride is now laughing.)
Miranda /
(Her shoulders shake.)
Oh / Miranda / you bitch in meringue / you
whore in confectionery / I could lick / I could
swallow / I could vomit you /

LUX: They let us through /

STURDEE: They let you through / this is only the first sign
of their profound capacity for mischief /

THE TRAIN: *(A nervous delight.)* They clapped /

STURDEE: They do / they do clap / and as they
disembowel you / they clap that too /
(The train frowns.)
But I am allowing my taste for the incongruous
to dismay these children / who / recruited to
this preposterous extravaganza by an infantile
vulgarity excusable in them / if not in you /
cannot be expected to know me as you do /
Miranda /
(He pretends to comfort the train.)
Nothing I say is true / nothing / so / when it
happens / shut your eyes / it's a bad dream /
(He permits himself a smile.)
Run away / sit in the corner / I've things to
say to your mistress she'd deem unsuitable / I
daresay / for your ears /
*(The train, relinquishing its posts, drifts away and
collects in a corner. From their obscurity the children
study STURDEE, fingers in their mouths.)*
The body / it kills us / the body /

LUX: It's meant to /

STURDEE: Yes / but you know me / I never do what I am
          told to do / by man or nature / instinct or the
          police / and I was winning /

LUX: Winning? / what were you winning / Sturdee? /

STURDEE: The argument /

LUX: What argument is this? /

STURDEE: *(Irritably.)* The argument with the body / I was
          winning it /
          (He regards her.)
          I got the body where I wanted it / comic /
          repulsive / a thing grotesquely ugly or decayed
          / I smell you / by the way / you / not the
          perfume you are smothered in / laughter
          played a part / you know how laughter comes
          to the aid of desperate men / and then / as if
          to thwart me / the body swims back in / not
          any body / the perfect body / the odd broken
          vein notwithstanding / and in this waterfall of
          splashing silk / this wave of satin / this fountain
          of brocade /
          (He bites his lip.)
          Immediately / the argument looks thin / and
          ridicule / a thing I reach for without proper
          consideration / it could be said / ridicule's a twig
          / snap /
          (He smiles.)
          Broken twig /
          (He regards her.)
          If Heaven has a smell / it's your skin / Miranda
          /
          (She regards him.)
          Strip your arse for me to kiss / they're coming
          / there's no time for bed / and bed is for the
          husband / obviously / who is the husband? /
          you never said /
          (LUX declines to reply.)
          A singer / an athlete / a philologist / you are
          hard / Miranda /

(She shakes her head.)
Yes / hard as brick / and therefore brittle /
(She shakes her head vigorously.)
Miranda / I admire it / soft women never
moved me /
*(LUX, forcing a decision on herself, snaps her fingers at
the train. The children emerge from the shadows.)*
I see / this visit / if it is a visit / was undertaken
purely to torture me /
(The children lift the train of the dress.)
Hurry now / or the chauffeur / when you find
him / may have no head /
(The children frown.)
His sense of direction will be compromised /
a crazy journey / up the pavement / leaping
lights / pouring down the wrong side of the
carriageway / impossible / you say / perhaps /
*(He creates a smile. LUX stares at him. The train
waits on her, apprehensive.)*

LUX: This visit /

STURDEE: If it is a visit /

LUX: *(Closing her eyes in irritation.)* It is a visit / Sturdee
           / yes / and it was undertaken not for you /

STURDEE: Me? / no /

LUX: Neither to please / nor wound you / believe
           me / and what you have taken from it / apart
           from indulging your appetite for cruelty / both
           to these children / and to me / was entirely
           predictable / and of no interest to me / I needed
           to see / before I went to my husband / the
           poverty of the thing I so long suffered / and
           this you demonstrated perfectly / for that I'm
           grateful /
           *(LUX allows her hardest stare to penetrate STURDEE.
           He reveals nothing. LUX gestures to the train. They lift
           the heavy satin and march from the room. STURDEE
           resumes an absolute immobility. OLIM appears in the
           shadows.)*

OLIM: Was that them? /
        (STURDEE ignores her.)
        They didn't stay / then? /
        *(She withdraws. As before, the great room fills with
        silence. At its most intense, it is exploded by the
        hysteria of the train, which rushes back into the room
        and like a flock of shrieking and maddened starlings,
        proceeds to climb onto STURDEE as if he were the last
        rock in an inundated landscape. The children wail,
        and fall, and hoist themselves again, a cacophony of
        terror which rises to a crescendo on the appearance
        of two male strangers who drag LUX backwards over
        the floor by the rope of her train, a return as ugly as
        her parting was dignified. They stop. Connoisseurs in
        chaos, they savour the atmosphere. The storm subsides.
        A tangible apprehension follows. STURDEE, invisible
        under the clinging children, is nevertheless audible.)*

STURDEE: It's all right / it's a dream /
        *(The strangers, made aware of STURDEE, abandon
        LUX and stroll to the clotted chair. STURDEE's feet
        protrude. The first stranger makes a feint at the
        children, who scramble away, screeching, and collect in
        a corner. STURDEE, revealed, sees his antagonists for
        the first time.)*
        Chaos stinks / these kids / I'm drenched /
        (The strangers contemplate the spectacle of STURDEE.)
        You're thinking / this bastard has a hundred
        suits / so one's pissed on / switch it for another
        / cream / beige / summer-weight / this thick
        blue serge / depressing / I agree with you / but
        it takes more than a war to break my habits / the
        new / I never liked it / but I should / I should
        do / it's here to stay / by the way / I said no to
        the shotgun /
        (He affects an intimate tone.)
        I was offered one / two if I wanted / I waved
        him away / who / did you say? / some killer /

267

talking of smells / you aren't so fragrant / either
/
(A pause. Then the SECOND STRANGER laughs.
STURDEE joins in.)
Gardens /
(He creates a dismissive gesture.)
I can't help thinking they spoil us for one
another / the sounds / the scents / flesh is
nauseating by comparison /
(He smiles swiftly.)
Dead / is she? / the bride? / fifty metres / she
told me / fifty / silk organza / the epitome of
artificiality / mind you / it works / one look at
her / you're on your knees / dead / or not? / I
can't see / arthritis / can't turn my head / what
did he say / the specialist? / mobility reduced
to twelve degrees / twelve degrees / not such a
handicap in times like these / the less you see
the better /
(The strangers laugh.)
You agree /
(He chuckles. The laughter fades.)
They said you were coming / every day /
'they're coming' / 'they're coming' / I was
sceptical / to begin with / then I got bored /
the rumour / in its own way / it makes you
impatient / same with death / 'show yourself' /
you want to say / all this loitering on the stairs
/ the threats / the menaces / get on with it / are
you staying? / is she dead? / too many questions
/ know less / know less / Sturdee /
(He creates a laugh, of a self-deprecating kind. A
fractional hiatus.)
You don't say much / but I inhibit you / my
volubility / you can't get a word in / it's nerves /
of course / but not entirely nerves / you're in my
house / not by invitation / but let's not quibble

over etiquette / I am the host / you two / you're
guests / naturally I pass the time of day / I /
(STURDEE is cut short by a terrible wail which comes
from LUX. It decays into a low sobbing. STURDEE lifts
his gaze to the strangers. They in turn scrutinize him.)

DEMONSTRATOR: Women / when I think of them / I think
of noise / giggling / shrieking / weeping / at
school I dreaded playtime / I covered my ears /
I covered my eyes / the yelling of the girls / the
ugly mischief of the boys / and then the sexual
act / a rehearsal I assume / for birth / I see no
need for it / I see no need for animal sounds
when we have words /
(He has not removed his eyes from STURDEE.)
Sturdee /
(STURDEE is circumspect.)

STURDEE: I'll mention it / in case she /
(He frowns.)
Erupts again /
(DEMONSTRATOR maintains his scrutiny of
STURDEE, who for the first time looks away, a
concession he at once regrets and lifts his eyes again.)
I don't agree / words / exquisite artefacts of
culture as they are / fail sometimes / and fail
beautifully / to be lost for words / on rare
occasions / is a testament to our capacity for /
(He shrugs.)
Love / say /

DEMONSTRATOR: Or horror /

STURDEE: Horror / yes /

DEMONSTRATOR: Sturdee / quarrel if you want / debate with
me / but what you want you cannot have / I
think you know that already /
(STURDEE is disingenuous.)

STURDEE: What? / What do I want I cannot have? /

DEMONSTRATOR: Ascendancy /
(He casts a glance at the SECOND STRANGER.)

Pull her here / Sturdee's vertebrae seize after
twelve degrees / and he must see /
*(The SECOND STRANGER goes to LUX and grabbing
the train of her dress proceeds to pull her over the floor.
LUX cries out.)*

STURDEE: *(At his most resonant.)* Miranda /
(She howls.)
HE HATES NOISE /
(LUX is dragged to DEMONSTRATOR's feet.)
Women's noise / particularly /
*(LUX obeys STURDEE's injunction. She lies on her
back in the mass of her satin, as STURDEE, craning
his neck as far as it will go, attempts to settle the
children as one might calm dogs.)*
Bad dream / bad dream /
*(They also settle. DEMONSTRATOR regards them with
distaste.)*

DEMONSTRATOR: It's not the playground / is it? /

STURDEE: It's not a playground / certainly / it's my home /

DEMONSTRATOR: *(A new tone.)* I said / you may not have it /

STURDEE: I may not have it / no /

DEMONSTRATOR: What may you not have / Sturdee? /

STURDEE: I may not have ascendancy /
(DEMONSTRATOR stares, then falters.)

DEMONSTRATOR: I apologize / how coarse that was / the
manner of a corporal / to make you say my own
word back to me /

STURDEE: I accept your apology / as for the word / it's /
(He affects modesty.)
not your property / I'm always saying it / ask
Miranda /
*(LUX, who has been flat on her back since she
was dragged into the room, sits up, the image of
dishevelment. She looks boldly at DEMONSTRATOR.)*

LUX: Darling /
(She screws up her face.)
Oh / darling /
(She makes a futile effort to rise to her feet.)

I'll wash my face / my face is all / I'll wash my face /

STURDEE: *(Gravely.)* Miranda /

LUX: Miranda / Miranda / my face is wrecked / how can he love me? /
(She struggles. She is caught in her train. She collapses. She stops struggling. She laughs, a deep, strange sound.)
Come on / then /
(And laughs.)
Come on / come on to me /
(DEMONSTRATOR regards her with contempt.)
Brides cry / you know brides / wet through /

STURDEE: *(Perceiving DEMONSTRATOR's mood.)* Miranda /

LUX: Miranda / Miranda / I do think you / especially you / would do well to /
(She shudders. She looks to DEMONSTRATOR.)
It's the way he says Miranda / I feel sure you will say Miranda differently /
(DEMONSTRATOR's gaze is cold but fixed. LUX whilst talking to STURDEE, does not take her eyes off her antagonist.)
He slew my husband / kill won't do / he slew / the word is beautiful / say slew / say slew /
(DEMONSTRATOR is silent. MIRANDA laughs her deepest laugh, then chokes it. A darkness suffuses her.)
When you slay a husband / the bride / what is that word? / the bride /
(She screws up her fists.)
DEVOLVES /
(She laughs swiftly.)
THE BRIDE DEVOLVES ON YOU /
(She is lascivious, cruel.)
Come on to me /
(STURDEE senses disaster, and to break the tension calls out to the children.)

STURDEE: Bad dream / bad dream / wake up soon /

LUX: *(Seizing on the idea.)* Call them / call the children / they can't see / the / oh /
(Again she tightens her fists.)
second word escaping me / what is it / Sturdee / when the husband comes onto the wife / and she /

STURDEE: Consummation /

LUX: CONSUMMATION / YES / THEY HAVE TO SEE MY DARLING STRIP THE GOWN OFF ME /
(LUX's intensity deepens the bitterness of DEMONSTRATOR, as STURDEE anticipated.)

DEMONSTRATOR: You do not hear your ancestors / do you? / and they are calling / from some deep pit of history / saying / kneel now / lower your eyes / but you do not kneel / or know how to / everything that saves the weak / you despise / your complacency offends me /
(He looks to the second stranger.)
Take the children to the garden / Mr Sturdee / quite properly / reminds us / we are guests / we will be scrupulous / therefore / and not lend him the opportunity to criticize us / for shedding blood under his roof / then come back / and do / I don't know / whatever occurs to you / to this / this / whatever / this / arrogant and / I don't know / this /
(He makes a swift, angry gesture.)
GET THEM OUT / GET THEM OUT /

STURDEE: She is arrogant / she is / she is arrogant whilst / at the same time / peculiarly susceptible to guilt / unhealthy I admit /
(The SECOND STRANGER is advancing on the children, who shrink. With a supreme effort, STURDEE lifts himself out of his chair.)
THE GARDEN IS NOT LESS SACRED /
(The second stranger is briefly distracted.)

DEMONSTRATOR: Very well / do it in the street /

(STURDEE, hanging in the air, is speechless. DEMONSTRATOR watches him, with a zoological objectivity. For a fraction of a second there is pure silence in the room. Then the children scream, running in all directions, as the SECOND STRANGER plunges after them, blocking them, heading them off. In the midst of the chaos, STURDEE is a spectacle of disbelief. At last the room is emptied.)

STURDEE: I said no to the shotgun / I said no /
(He stares at LUX.)
I said no to the shotgun / no / I said /
(LUX is stricken, immobile. DEMONSTRATOR walks a few paces, apparently thoughtful.)

DEMONSTRATOR: Children / what are they? / yet-to-be fraudsters / yet-to-be whores / yet-to-be / yet-to-be /

STURDEE: Killers of children? /

DEMONSTRATOR: Everything you say is predictable / neither hatred / nor rage / delivers you / from this predictability / which disappoints me / not because I entertained some little hope it might be otherwise / but in case I am the same /

STURDEE: Be predictable / Mr / Mr /
(He is puzzled.)
Strange / I don't know your name /

DEMONSTRATOR: Demonstrator /

STURDEE: Demonstrator? / is that a name? /
(DEMONSTRATOR casts a withering glance at STURDEE.)
Hurt me / Mr Demonstrator / let the kids go /
(DEMONSTRATOR goes to STURDEE, scrutinizing him.)

DEMONSTRATOR: Do you mean that? /

STURDEE: I /
(He reflects.)
Yes / I think so / I /
(He affirms.)

Yes / because the pain of the children / and of
their parents / the sheer volume of pain / put
against mine / oh / it's /
(He looks at DEMONSTRATOR.)

DEMONSTRATOR: *(With contempt.)* That's arithmetic /
*(STURDEE sinks back into the chair. OLIM enters,
horrified, half-clothed.)*

OLIM: Something's happening in the road /

STURDEE: Yes /

OLIM: *(Seeing DEMONSTRATOR and LUX.)* Sturdee /

STURDEE: Yes / I said / yes / yes /
(OLIM stares, perched on her stick.)
It is arithmetic / to some extent / more pain is
worse / presumably / than less? /

DEMONSTRATOR: Your logic nauseates me / Mr Sturdee /
(He casts a glance at OLIM.)
And you / go back to bed /

OLIM: *(Defiantly.)* This is my own home /

DEMONSTRATOR: Is that so? / from now on / in your own
home / you dress /
(LUX peels with laughter.)

OLIM: *(To STURDEE, as the truth dawns on her.)* They're
here / they're here / then? /

STURDEE: That's right / they're here /
(He resuscitates his argument.)
Your contempt for logic / I can't help noticing /
is selective / guns and things / tanks / bombs /
etcetera / you are oddly tolerant of /
(He alters.)
WASTING MY BREATH / WASTING MY
BREATH /
*(The SECOND STRANGER enters, oddly calm. He
looks at LUX, strewn as before with fabrics.)*

SONG: I got five / and one ran off /

OLIM: *(Struggling to comprehend.)* Five? /

SONG: Five / and one ran off /

OLIM: *(Deepening.)* FIVE? / FIVE? /

SONG: *(Brutally.)* AND ONE RAN OFF /

STURDEE: Miss Olim finds the killing of children
incomprehensible / you mustn't be angry with
her / what is perfectly natural to you / even
routine / fills her with disbelief / she reels / she
rocks / she has / in most regards / enjoyed a
sheltered life /
(SONG goes to LUX and climbs onto her.)
And that / despite her beauty / I don't hesitate
to affirm Miss Olim was / and remained / longer
than most who might have commanded the title
/ the most beautiful woman in the world / I'm
not exaggerating /
*(SONG rapes LUX. DEMONSTRATOR watches with a
clinical regard.)*
Whilst conceding it is / strictly speaking /
impossible to be categorical in issuing claims of a
universal nature / I am prepared to state / there
was not a woman in the world / *more* beautiful
than Olim / she possessed / after all / not only
the physical attributes of beauty / some of which
may have been reproduced in some remote place
/ I don't deny the possibility / a village in Peru / a
slum in Sicily / but in addition / a thing unlikely
to be encountered in the wider world / Olim
had poise / and poise is nine-parts of beauty / I
exaggerate / not nine / let's say / beauty without
poise cannot create in us that awesome / and
annihilating / sense of the divine / inspired by the
perfect body / the perfect face / and the perfect
culture in which these phenomena are registered
/ notwithstanding the form of this perfection is
itself unstable / corruptible / and likely to be
replaced by others /
*(STURDEE falters. SONG is briefly limp. LUX is
resolutely silent.)*
Equally liable to decay /
(STURDEE stares.)
And so on /

(A profound stillness.)

Miranda / you are wonderful / Miranda /

OLIM: Miranda? / Miranda who? /

DEMONSTRATOR: *(As SONG staggers up.)* Now kill her /

STURDEE: *(Inspired by horror.)* I wonder if / Heaven forbid
I should encourage it / I wonder if you ever do
these acts yourself / Mr Demonstrator / or if it is
sufficient to be only implicated? /

OLIM: Miranda who? /

STURDEE: *(Ignoring OLIM.)* Presumably the satisfaction / if it
is satisfying / derives from /

OLIM: MIRANDA WHO? /

STURDEE: *(Provoked and venomous.)* MIRANDA WHO?
/ MIRANDA WHO? / MIRANDA WHO
MADE ME SING / AND SULK / AND
SUFFER / AND OF WHOSE EXISTENCE
YOU KNEW NOTHING /

             (OLIM stares at STURDEE.)

             Albeit / her moods played on you like a second
weather /

             *(SONG grabs the train of LUX's now destroyed gown to
drag her from the room.)*

             No hurry / Mr / Mr / I don't think we were
introduced /

DEMONSTRATOR: Song /

STURDEE: Song? / is that a name? /

DEMONSTRATOR: It's his name /

STURDEE: Mr Song / I /

             *(STURDEE falters, and bursts into tears. Both SONG
and DEMONSTRATOR observe his misery with
detachment.)*

OLIM: Sturdee /

             *(OLIM's voice only serves to deepen STURDEE's
wretchedness. He howls. His shoulders heave.)*

             Sturdee /

DEMONSTRATOR: Mr Sturdee was near /

             (STURDEE wails.)

I say near / he was / in some regards / quite
near / to gaining an ascendancy over me /
sensing this / I was obliged to invoke the
concept even as it threatened me / in order to
render it innocuous / that is how close he came
to his intention /

STURDEE: *(Bawling at SONG.)* I'LL KILL YOU /

DEMONSTRATOR: Alas /

STURDEE: KILL YOU I SAID /

DEMONSTRATOR: It's dissipated now /
          (He takes a step towards STURDEE.)
          You know my attitude to noise / Mr Sturdee /
          how I do not like to hear expletives / threats /
          ejaculations /

STURDEE: I do know / yes /

DEMONSTRATOR: When we have created / between us / an
          almost meditative atmosphere / it is particularly
          hurtful to discover you are / for all your powers
          of objectivity and articulation / a frustrated lout
          when you sense you have lost command of the
          situation /

STURDEE: It's pitiful /

DEMONSTRATOR: And this despite the proximity of a garden
          which /

STURDEE: She does the garden /

DEMONSTRATOR: Conventionally / at least / is an antidote to
          coarse behaviour /

STURDEE: She does it / the garden / not me /
          (A fractional hiatus.)
          Still / I agree / this is not a tenement in a slum /
          my outburst was /
          (He waves a hand dismissively.)
          An outburst / and / inconsistent with the
          tranquillity engendered by this rural idyll / I
          apologize to Mr Song / his job is hard enough /
          surely / without his being subjected to threats /
          abuse / etcetera / by the likes of me /

OLIM: Sturdee / it's redundant /

STURDEE: What is? /
OLIM: The method /
STURDEE: Method? /
OLIM: They don't hear irony / the thousand years
                  of culture in your language / your blend of
                  melancholy and disdain / beg instead /
                  (She turns to DEMONSTRATOR.)
                  You would prefer that / wouldn't you? /
                  unfortunately he has no legs / he can't go down
                  but /
DEMONSTRATOR: *(To SONG.)* Leave her /
SONG: *(Puzzled.)* Leave her? /
DEMONSTRATOR: That one / leave her / kill this one instead /
STURDEE: *(An eruption.)* YOU DO IT / YOU DO
                  IT / ALWAYS TELLING HIM / DO IT
                  YOURSELF /
OLIM: No one lays a finger on me /
                  *(SONG, obediently, abandons LUX and advances on
                  OLIM.)*
STURDEE: That's not begging /
OLIM: *(Raising her cane.)* I will give him such a smack /
STURDEE: Is it? /
OLIM: *(To SONG.)* Get back / you dog / you stink / you
                  animal / get back /
STURDEE: I don't call that begging / but as Mr
                  Demonstrator says / we've lost the knack / all
                  these centuries / property / authority / the army
                  / and the law /
                  *(SONG grabs OLIM's cane in a swift gesture. She cries
                  out, covering her face with her hands.)*
                  MR SONG / I'LL LICK THE SHIT OUT OF
                  YOUR CRACK /
                  (He shuts his eyes in his desperation.)
                  PLEASE / PLEASE /
                  (He shakes his head.)
DEMONSTRATOR: That word /
STURDEE: What word? /
DEMONSTRATOR: Please /

STURDEE: Have I not said the word before? /

DEMONSTRATOR: No / Sturdee / and in a civil war / please is
             perfect / as is sorry /

STURDEE: Sorry? / sorry / yes / sorry / what am I sorry
             for? /
             (DEMONSTRATOR is patient.)
             I'm sorry /

DEMONSTRATOR: *(To OLIM.)* Lie on the floor /

STURDEE: I SAID I'M SORRY /

OLIM: It's all right / Sturdee /

STURDEE: *(Smothering his face in his hands.)* OH / DON'T /
             OH / DON'T / MY DEAR LOVE / DON'T /
             (LUX begins to laugh hysterically.)

OLIM: *(To SONG.)* Give me your arm /

STURDEE: OH / DON'T / OH / DON'T /

OLIM: *(To SONG, who is sneering.)* I can't get down / if
             you don't help /
             *(SONG casts a glance towards demonstrator, who
             tosses his head brutally. SONG thrusts OLIM down.
             She cries out as she collapses.)*

SONG: Next time / say please / like Mr Sturdee does /
             (LUX laughs. OLIM shakes her head defiantly.)

DEMONSTRATOR: Fuck her /

STURDEE: *(A howl.)* HURT ME / HURT ME /

DEMONSTRATOR: We are / aren't we? / we are hurting you /
             now / beg Mr Song / Say / Mr Song / fuck my
             wife / please /
             *(A profound hiatus. LUX ceases laughing. STURDEE
             looks into DEMONSTRATOR. OLIM breaks the silence.)*

OLIM: Say it / Sturdee /

STURDEE: Say it? /

OLIM: Say the words / Sturdee /
             (STURDEE's face is a mask of reluctance.)

DEMONSTRATOR: Sturdee / who has the ascendancy? /

STURDEE: You /

DEMONSTRATOR: Me / I have it / and how do I have it? /

STURDEE: How do you have it? / God knows /

DEMONSTRATOR: Do I have it wholly / or partially? /

STURDEE: You have it wholly /
DEMONSTRATOR: WHOLLY / YES / WHOLE AND
            ABSOLUTE IS MY ASCENDANCY /
            (He suddenly shrugs.)
            You make me childish / say the words / out loud
            / enunciate them properly /
STURDEE: I'm sorry I make you childish / possibly you /
OLIM: *(Admonishing him.)* Sturdee /
            (With a deeply drawn breath, STURDEE speaks.)
STURDEE: Mr Song /
            (He bites his lip.)
            Mr Song /
            *(His head trembles. DEMONSTRATOR watches, both
            ecstatic and appalled.)*
            Fuck my wife / please /
            (Swiftly.)
            SHE'S NOT MY WIFE /
            (OLIM laughs with an acute bitterness.)
OLIM: I'm not his wife / he wouldn't marry me /
DEMONSTRATOR: The most beautiful woman in the world /
            and still he /
OLIM: Prevaricated /
DEMONSTRATOR: If it's any consolation / Mr Song / will not
            think twice /
STURDEE: Or once / presumably? /
DEMONSTRATOR: Or once / I compare him to a dog /
            characterized by two things / appetite / and
            loyalty /
            (He turns to SONG.)
            Mr Sturdee has implored you to rape the
            woman who is not his wife / I do think we must
            satisfy him / if only to reward his hospitality /
            after that / castrate him / he must not be allowed
            to think he can indulge these perverse desires
            with impunity /
STURDEE: WHY DON'T YOU / ONCE IN A WHILE /
            JUST ONCE / DO YOUR OWN ATROCITY /
            (SONG falls to raping OLIM.)

THIS FASTIDIOUS DETACHMENT IT'S /

OLIM: *(Agonized.)* STURDEE /

STURDEE: IT'S /

OLIM: STURDEE /

STURDEE: CAN'T SEE / OLIM /

DEMONSTRATOR: Mr Sturdee's neck / I remember now /
rotates no more than twelve degrees /
(He goes to SONG.)
Stop now / stop / stop /
(SONG is impervious to instructions.
DEMONSTRATOR looks bemused.)
Didn't I say / Song's a dog / half-appetite /
(He grasps SONG by his hair.)
STOP / I SAID /
(SONG is fixed.)
Half-loyalty / now shift Mr Sturdee's chair / so
he can see /
(SONG climbs to his feet, leaden.)
Alternatively / drag her here /
(SONG is disoriented. He looks one way, then the
other.)
One / or the other / the point is / Mr Sturdee
must be gratified / you recollect / he asked for
this / politely / he said please / so if we simply /
and selfishly /
(SONG goes to STURDEE's chair and turns it.)
Thank you / and now / proceed /
(SONG looks recalcitrant.)
Kiss her /
(SONG hesitates.)
Kiss now /
(SONG kneels over OLIM. He is unwilling. He draws
his hand across his mouth.)
You will offend her / and what is worse / offend
Sturdee / whose lifelong love she is /
(SONG shakes his head.)

STURDEE: She fills him with disgust /

DEMONSTRATOR: Evidently /

STURDEE: Her mouth all fallen in / her ruined skin / the flesh runs off her bone like water / as if her whole substance was called to another place / by God / or gravity / nothing stays / nothing clings /

DEMONSTRATOR: KISS HER / ANYWHERE /

STURDEE: He can't / and he's a dog /
(SONG casts an angry glance at STURDEE.)

DEMONSTRATOR: I should not have stopped him /

STURDEE: That was a mistake / it gave him pause for thought /

DEMONSTRATOR: *(To SONG.)* Get up now /

STURDEE: Whereas in the first place some sordid mischief made her decay a positive inducement to him / it took only a fleeting moment of / one can scarcely call it objectivity /

DEMONSTRATOR: Get up / I said /

STURDEE: Nevertheless / a judgement of some kind / however dim / to make him recoil /
(SONG climbs to his feet.)
So what if she had been the most beautiful woman in the world? / she is no longer / what maddened me and ten thousand others dressed / now / stark naked / makes a dog creep to its corner / depressed / do I sound a moralist? / not in the least / the long run / Mr Demonstrator / let us say of the long run / whereas it has no morals / it does not lack for wit /
(STURDEE is surprised to see DEMONSTRATOR go to OLIM and with a certain tenderness lift her into his arms. Without a word, he carries her from the room. SONG looks at STURDEE.)

SONG: The kitchen / where is it? /
(STURDEE seems not to hear.)
The kitchen / Sturdee /

STURDEE: Downstairs /

SONG: Downstairs / is it /

STURDEE: *(As SONG goes.)* Mr Demonstrator / is he / does he /

SONG: I'm fucking starving /
             (SONG goes out.)

STURDEE: Yes / I can imagine / and he says kill / kill this
             / rape that / all very well / but on an empty
             stomach? /
             (An uncanny silence fills the room. STURDEE is alert
             to every sound, a mass of tightened nerves. At last LUX
             speaks from the corner where she was abandoned like a
             doll.)

LUX: I'm telling the police /
             (STURDEE ignores her.)
             STURDEE / I'M TELLING THE POLICE /

STURDEE: *(Patiently, as to a child.)* Yes / certainly the police
             should know /
             (He resumes his listening.)

LUX: I'm telling them / Sturdee /

STURDEE: *(Faintly irritated.)* Yes / when they come back /
             tell them /

LUX: *(Gravely.)* About us /
             (STURDEE's attention is focused swiftly by LUX's
             words.)

STURDEE: Us? /

LUX: Us / yes / you and me / us fucking / when I was
             13 /
             (STURDEE's head swims.)

STURDEE: That was 20 years ago / Miranda /

LUX: SO WHAT? / 20 YEARS / SO WHAT? / IT
             AFFECTED ME /

STURDEE: Discuss it later /

LUX: *(Sitting bolt upright.)* Not later / now / now /
             Sturdee /

STURDEE: Miranda /

LUX: *(Beating the floor with her fists.)* NOW / NOW /
             DISCUSS IT NOW / STURDEE /
             (She glares at the back of his head, fixed and
             intractable.)

I am the bride / today's my day / so everything
I say / you do / you do it nicely / and try not to
argue / all the time you argue /

STURDEE: Do I? /

LUX: Yes / you do /
(STURDEE concedes.)
Now / what did you think when you looked at
me? / a child of 13? / in little socks and little
shoes? / did you think / that kid is so innocent
she /

STURDEE: You weren't in socks /

LUX: YOU SEE / YOU SEE / ALWAYS YOU
ARGUE /

STURDEE: Miranda / we have recalled this moment / not
once /

LUX: ARGUE / AND ARGUE /

STURDEE: Not twice / not a hundred / but a thousand
times / and recalled it in a froth of ecstasy /
YOUR LEGS WERE BARE / LONG LEGS
AND BARE / THESE LONG BARE LEGS
CLUNG DESPERATELY TO ME /
(LUX erupts in sobbing.)
Shh /
(STURDEE strains his hearing against LUX's cries.)
Shh /

LUX: The police / Sturdee /

STURDEE: It's Olim /
(He heaves himself up, his neck agonized.)

LUX: I'll say you didn't mean to / I'll say I led you on
/ Sturdee /

STURDEE: MIRANDA / SHUT UP / PLEASE /

LUX: YOU HAVE TO BE PUNISHED / STURDEE
/ YOU HAVE TO BE /
*(She bites her lip. She snorts. The sound of OLIM's
pain or pleasure filters from an upstairs room.
STURDEE is a picture of fascination. LUX is also
attentive. SONG enters, eating from a dinner plate
piled with food.)*

STURDEE:	Mr Demonstrator /
	(He looks at SONG, who stands and chews.)
	What is he? /
	(SONG regards STURDEE with a bemused contempt.)
SONG:	I forgot to castrate you /
STURDEE:	*(Sinking into the seat.)* Oh / that can wait / surely? /
SONG:	I don't know if it can /
	(SONG chews, baiting STURDEE.)
	Not that it matters much / does it / to you? /
	(A sharp cry from above causes STURDEE to lift his head. SONG observes this. He casts a glance at LUX.)
	And killing her / we forgot that / too /
STURDEE:	Time for all these things /
SONG:	Get round to it / eventually /
STURDEE:	Lunch first / lunch is the priority / did you find all you wanted? /
	(SONG chews.)
	Olim / she eats like a bird / and me / I pick / so probably what we consume in a week represents a paltry snack to you /
	(SONG chews.)
	Mr Demonstrator / I imagine / is fastidious about food? / small portions / exquisitely prepared / a few choice items which /
SONG:	He likes you /
	(SONG chews. STURDEE bides his time.)
STURDEE:	Being liked by Mr Demonstrator / I daresay / does not preclude /
	(With a violent twist of his body, SONG flings the dinner plate against the wall. It shatters. STURDEE places his hands together, thoughtfully. SONG wipes his hands on his clothes. He goes to LUX.)
SONG:	I'm fucking you /
	(He proceeds to attack her. On this occasion LUX weeps audibly, her wretchedness inscribed on STURDEE's features, tightening his face into a mask of shame and hopelessness. At the worst point of his / LUX's misery,

*the girls erupt into the room, dancing grotesquely
and hysterical, a hideous chorus-line of violation and
dishevelment. As they cavort before STURDEE's aching
eyes, DEMONSTRATOR enters, towelling his hair, and
in STURDEE's dressing gown. He watches casually.
The girls collapse, and lie on the floor, a mess of limbs,
heaving and drenched.)*

DEMONSTRATOR: She's sleeping /
*(He proceeds to comb his hair. SONG, his act
completed, climbs to his feet. Again, the room fills with
silence.)*

STURDEE: I have this sense / peculiar and hallucinatory /
surely / that everything I am witnessing / if I am
witnessing / if it's not a dream / is happening
for me / to me / obviously / but for me / is
this normal with atrocity / I wonder / this /
quality of revelation / Mr Demonstrator? / I am
thinking / this is so vile / vile but also necessary
/
*(STURDEE succeeds in turning his head to
DEMONSTRATOR.)*
Compensation / probably / the ego on overtime
/

DOUGHTY/COADE: *(Sitting up abruptly.)* THAT'S HIM /
HE SHOULD BE KILLED / OH / THOSE
AWFUL WEDNESDAYS / WE WERE /
CAN'T SAY / MUST SAY / HORRIBLY
/ HORRIBLY / CAN'T SAY / MUST SAY
/ TORTURED / HUMILIATED / AND
DAMAGED / DAMAGED / IRREPARABLY
/ WEREN'T WE? /
*(They look at one another. DEMONSTRATOR puts
away his comb.)*

DEMONSTRATOR: You see / always there are those who
insist on regarding us as liberators / but we are
neither forensic / nor judicial / strictly speaking
whereas we hurt / we do not punish / it may be
/ of course / that some we hurt deserve it / or

all / all perhaps deserve it in the same degree /
but we cannot be hindered / or stimulated / by
such considerations / atrocity is / by definition /
unencumbered / what occurs on Wednesdays? /

DOUGHTY/COADE: OH / HE / OH / HE /

DEMONSTRATOR: Sturdee /

(The girls are silent.)

STURDEE: They dance /

(He regards DOUGHTY and COADE.)

And they are ugly / manifestly ugly /

DOUGHTY/COADE: *(Indignant.)* YOU SEE / YOU SEE
WHAT HE'S /

(SONG surges towards them. They shrink.)

STURDEE: They have no talent for dancing / obviously /

DOUGHTY/COADE: *(Stung and shrill.)* WE DO / WE DO
HAVE TALENT / ONLY HE /

(SONG raises a fist to them. They bite their lips.)

STURDEE: I insist they exaggerate their natural clumsiness /
the worse they dance / the more it pleases me /
and for this I reward them / inordinately / some
would say / this unearned wealth they spend on
drugs and lurid underwear /

*(The girls burst into tears. DEMONSTRATOR goes to
STURDEE and rests his hands on his shoulders.)*

DEMONSTRATOR: And this relieves you / this appalling
objectivity / whilst it humiliates them /
simultaneously / dignifies you / should they
castrate you / do you think? /

STURDEE: Possibly / if someone has to / that's my dressing
gown you're wearing / frayed cuffs / and greasy
collar / scruffy for you / but /

DEMONSTRATOR: How does it dignify you / Sturdee / to
subject these children / to an ordeal / the effects
of which / in the long term / might be crippling
to / what is / after all / the very delicate nature
of adolescent sexuality? /

*(STURDEE is speechless. In the silence, LUX
is seen to rise from the floor. Her head turns*

to DEMONSTRATOR, her face a mask of
incomprehension. STURDEE senses her.)

STURDEE: Miranda /
(Ignoring STURDEE, MIRANDA lifts a hand,
indicating DEMONSTRATOR. It hangs in the air.
She shakes her head in disbelief. STURDEE surpasses
himself.)
There's no contradiction here / no contradiction
/ if there appears to be / it's the distorting effect
of what he / Mr Demonstrator / describes /
quite properly / as the nauseating / character
of logic / to which we cling / so miserably /
as drowning men / to straws / etcetera / no /
crucially / crucially / we /
(The effort destroys STURDEE's coherence. LUX
struggles with her own hand. A terrible laugh comes
from her and she falls back into her ruined garments.)

DEMONSTRATOR: *(To SONG.)* Take these outside and kill them /
(DOUGHTY and COADE explode in tears. SONG waits
briefly, as if wanting confirmation of the order. When
it doesn't come, he goes to the girls to drag them out.)

STURDEE: *(Over the screams of the girls.)* WE ARE / WE
ARE / I THINK YOU MUST ADMIT /

DOUGHTY/COADE: STURDEE / STURDEE /

STURDEE: DOING OUR BEST / OUR VERY BEST
/ TO SHED THOSE / INGRAINED /
COMPLACENT / AND /

DOUGHTY/COADE: STURDEE SHOULD BE KILLED /
NOT US /

STURDEE: UN / UN /

DOUGHTY/COADE: KILL STURDEE / KILL STURDEE
PLEASE /

STURDEE: UN / UN /
(He shuts his eyes.)
I CANNOT CONCENTRATE /
(The girls are briefly silent.)

DEMONSTRATOR: I said this /

STURDEE: You did / not long ago / you said how sensitive you were to noise /

DEMONSTRATOR: The noise of women /

STURDEE: Women's noise / or girls /

DEMONSTRATOR: The more excited they become /

STURDEE: The more excruciating the pitch /
(He is inspired.)
UN / RE / COGITATED /
(He smiles.)
Our principles /
(He half-turns his head.)
UN / RE / COGITATED /
(Unseen by STURDEE, OLIM has entered the room.)
So much so / it might be said / they ceased to be principles / oh / long ago / and became instead / mere prejudices /
(He relentlessly pursues his thought.)
For example / what's it to me if these profoundly ugly / and ungifted / adolescents / are alive / or dead? /
(DEMONSTRATOR is silent, his hands resting still on STURDEE's shoulders.)
RE / COGITATE /
(He bites his lip.)
Then / and only then / when we have dismantled the mechanism of our attitudes / cleaned every part / and like some patient minder of machinery / reassembled it / could it be said /
(He looks at DOUGHTY/COADE.)
WE AUTHENTICALLY PROTEST /
(In the silence, OLIM advances, stickless and with a nearly-natural gait. Sensing her authority the girls plead.)

DOUGHTY/COADE: Miss Olim / Miss Olim /

OLIM: Shh /

DOUGHTY/COADE: Oh / Miss Olim /

OLIM: It's better / sometimes / to let the thing that
        threatens you come nearer / and not to bawl /
        and not to beg / because there is an afterwards /
        and even if you are not in this afterwards / still /
        this afterwards exists and will be defined by your
        manner of having abandoned it /
        (The girls look dimly at OLIM.)

DEMONSTRATOR: *(Kindly to OLIM.)* I left you sleeping /

OLIM: A beautiful sleep / thank you /

STURDEE: *(Provoked.)* It's the long run / the long run again
        / unfortunately / this concept of the afterwards /
        so perfectly articulated by Miss Olim / lives only
        in consciousness / and as she says / you won't
        have consciousness / not after Mr Song has
        taken off your head /
        (He looks to OLIM.)
        How do you mean / a beautiful sleep? / it's ten
        years since you slept / or stood without a stick /
        for that matter /
        (A peel of laughter comes from LUX.)
        Yes / it's funny / very funny / but I am
        beginning to sense a certain / how should
        I describe it? / the antithesis of logic / an
        aesthetic / let us say / governing the apparently
        arbitrary nature of Mr Demonstrator's acts /
        the savage orchestra makes music / this music
        / a cacophony to us / is nevertheless composed
        and played according to some law / Olim is
        entranced with Mr Demonstrator / who has
        restored her / but the fact she can now walk
        unaided / sleep divinely / and / if I heard
        correctly through the floor / sweetly fuck /
        should not blind her to the likelihood her master
        has yet more terrible punishments in store / for
        her / for all of us /

OLIM: Sturdee / you are a defeated man / you were
        born defeated / even as you left your mother's
        womb / it smothered you / like a caul /

DEMONSTRATOR: All the same / Mr Sturdee has identified
an aspect of things never apparent to those who
cling to hope or trust in luck /

STURDEE: Luck / no / bad luck / that's reliable /

OLIM: You see / you see /

DEMONSTRATOR: Simply ascribing everything one finds
appalling to the arbitrary is / once the shock of
the spectacle has evaporated / frustrating and
inadequate / bewilderment is the privilege of
the victim / no / a mind so keen as Mr Sturdee's
could never be satisfied with that / he is perhaps
on the brink of an agonizing perception /
but one so cruel it might be generous of us to
forestall by / for example / cutting his throat /
(STURDEE laughs mildly, without affectation.)

DOUGHTY/COADE: CUT IT / CUT IT / CUT HIS THROAT
/

OLIM: Shut up / you ugly bitches /
*(LUX laughs shrilly. DEMONSTRATOR visibly recoils
from the noise, and signals with his head to song that
he should drag the girls out of the room.)*

STURDEE: I was right / then / everything that is happening
/ is happening / for me / there is no possibility
that Mr Song will cut my throat / I am the
subject of everything that happens / and the
subject / it goes without saying / the subject /
must be seen to see /
(He booms at the girls.)
YOUR NOISE / YOUR NOISE / IS / SPOILING
EVERYBODY'S CONCENTRATION / MR
DEMONSTRATOR / HE /
(STURDEE falters.)
Has so much to think of /
(He looks to SONG.)
It's true / isn't it / Mr Song? / you would find it /
not repugnant exactly / but profoundly /
(He chooses the word.)
Heretical / to injure me? /

SONG: *(Grimly.)* I could hurt you / Mr Sturdee /

STURDEE: You could do / obviously / but /

SONG: I like your face /

STURDEE: You like my face / you see / there is always
a reason to desist / the weather / the state of
his digestion / my physiognomy / reasons in
profusion / the real reason / however /
(STURDEE is suddenly reluctant to continue.)
The real reason / for all that Mr Demonstrator
squirms to admit it / is that I have acquired a
certain / ascendancy /
(He looks at DEMONSTRATOR.)
An ascendancy I never would have chosen / a
hideous ascendancy / and everyone is going to
be sacrificed to it /

DEMONSTRATOR: It's true / you bring out the worst in me /

STURDEE: I know I do /

DEMONSTRATOR: Something vulgar /

STURDEE: Really? /

DEMONSTRATOR: Something pornographic / self-
consciousness / possibly /
*(The meditation causes DEMONSTRATOR intense
discomfort. To abolish it, he issues a wild instruction.)*
Take the skin off these /
*(He tosses his head towards the girls. SONG, caught
momentarily off-guard, frowns.)*
Flay them /
(The girls blanch, briefly speechless.)
In the road / tie them to trees / and flay them /

DOUGHTY/COADE: *(As if from the grave.)* WE DANCE / WE
DANCE / WE ONLY DANCE / DON'T WE? /

OLIM: *(Remonstrating with DEMONSTRATOR.)* Darling /

STURDEE: *(Sensing the futility.)* Olim /

OLIM: Darling / if I could say a word /

STURDEE: OLIM /

DEMONSTRATOR: *(Turning swiftly on her.)* Then her / her skin's
half-quit her bones already /

(SONG takes a girl in each fist and drags them from the room. LUX, delirious, sits upright and delivers a torrent of shame and ecstasy.)

LUX: Get down from the table / you rude little / you insolent little / get down / get down / or I will slap your legs /

OLIM: *(Aghast.)* FLAY ME? /

LUX: Slap them / slap your legs / Miranda / you rude little / you insolent little / slap you / slap your legs /

OLIM: FLAY? / ME? /

LUX: OW / MY THIGH IS RED / OW / OW /
(She laughs hysterically.)
She's on the bed / she flings herself / Miranda flings herself over the bed / dolls / annuals / in the air / a mess /
(She imitates a loving call.)
MIR – ANDA / MIR – ANDA / she blocks her ears / pillows / blankets / smothers her head / MIR – ANDA /
(She bawls.)
IF YOU WANT MIRANDA / YOU MUST BEG / AND /
(She laughs brightly.)
THEY DO / THEY BEG /

OLIM: *(To DEMONSTRATOR, who is half-attentive.)* You're not serious /

LUX: Mummy / Daddy / how they beg /

OLIM: Darling? /

LUX: They plead / they cringe / Miranda's head is under the pillows /
(OLIM lets out a cry of despair.)
But her legs / THOSE RED AND FLAMING SMACKS / Miranda darling / please come back /

OLIM: *(Trapped.)* Stick / stick /

LUX: Send Mr Sturdee / says Miranda / send Mr Sturdee up / if Mr Sturdee's nice / I'll come down for supper / BUT NOT OTHERWISE /

(LUX laughs.)

She lies / she lies in darkness listening for the
stairs / they creak / his voice / POOR DOLLS /
HE SAYS / POOR BEARS /
(She erupts in confused sobbing and laughter.)

OLIM: *(Paralyzed.)* OH / STICK / OH / STICK /

LUX: *(In a stillness.)* Immensely altered we /
descended / immensely altered /
*(As OLIM sobs, the distant sounds of the girls can
be heard, wailing. DEMONSTRATOR listens, as if a
connoisseur of distressed utterance.)*
Immensely / immensely / altered / we /

DEMONSTRATOR: Shh /

LUX: We /

DEMONSTRATOR: Be quiet / I said /
*(He takes a few steps, entranced. He looks to LUX, and
to STURDEE. The distant cries rise and fall.)*
I sometimes sense / at those rare moments when
I am tired / or feel I have done enough /
(He smiles wanly.)
And I admit / with an activity such as this / it is
never possible to identify what constitutes *enough*
/ one is sometimes satiated / but as Sturdee
knows better than all of us / to be satiated is not
the same as having had enough / it is merely a
pause / at such moments I detect some failure
on my part / as if I had not sufficiently exerted
my imagination / and whole corridors were
locked against me / deep shafts of inspiration
I lacked the will to penetrate / frustrating
obviously / and typical of the artistic personality
/ I am obliged to remind myself that / however
I fall short of those exacting standards I have set
myself / still / I am required / the quality may
falter / what is constant / is the need /
(He frowns.)
This enables me to carry on / even to exceed /
the limit /

(Distant sounds of pain and despair.)

STURDEE: Strange you should /

DEMONSTRATOR: *(Anticipating STURDEE.)* Yes /

STURDEE: Invoke the idea of the limit when /

DEMONSTRATOR: Yes / yes / I know what you are going to say / how should I speak of the *limit* / when I have so effectively abolished the concept of *enough?* / Sturdee is sharper than a pencil / no amount of misery can blunt the dark lead of his curiosity /

(He observes OLIM making pitiful progress from the room.)

Stay where you are /

OLIM: *(Feebly.)* Darling /

DEMONSTRATOR: On the contrary / if anything / it puts a finer point on it /

OLIM: Darling / I have to go to bed /

DEMONSTRATOR: This way you call me darling /

OLIM: I'm sorry / I'm so sorry /

DEMONSTRATOR: Persist with it if you wish /

OLIM: I apologize / I /

DEMONSTRATOR: It is as if / uttering the word conferred some dignity on our encounter / even to the extent of making a property of it / a property ¡ which you / and subsequently I / had made significant investment /

STURDEE: *(Bemused.)* Yes / yes /

DEMONSTRATOR: This is not the case /

OLIM: I am so sorry /

DEMONSTRATOR: Please / no more apology / ' to go to bed /

OLIM: I ache / I am a woman of 70

DEMONSTRATOR: Never / never again /

STURDEE: It's perfectly true what Mr

(OLIM screws up her face.)

OLIM: I AM IN SUCH PAIN / M DEMONSTRATOR /

STURDEE: Darling is a word of infinite reversibility / no / not reversibility / precisely / though let us admit / most of us have heard it / or used it / in a form entirely lacking love /
(OLIM sobs.)
There is / for all its spontaneity / an element of profound / almost zoological / calculation in it / an ejaculation / yes / but simultaneously / a claim / a contract issued in the same breath as an overwhelming love / darling /

OLIM: You know nothing / Sturdee /
(LUX laughs.)

STURDEE: *(Tasting the word.)* Darling /

OLIM: *(Bitterly, to LUX.)* Yes / and I know nothing / either /

DEMONSTRATOR: Your last recriminations / who undressed whom / and when / the tuneless dirge of your confessed and unconfessed betrayals /
(He shakes his head complacently.)
I think to flay the skin from men and women for whom skin was the stained and slippery substance of a false religion is / you must admit / entirely apposite / it's slow / however /
(He goes to leave.)
And Song has no /
(He shrugs his shoulders.)

STURDEE: Method? /

DEMONSTRATOR: He brings nothing to it /

STURDEE: I noticed that /

DEMONSTRATOR: Brutality / of course /

STURDEE: Yes /

DEMONSTRATOR: Brutality without knowledge /

STURDEE: Ordinary is Mr Song /

DEMONSTRATOR: Ordinary / yes /
(DEMONSTRATOR looks deeply into STURDEE.)
You cannot hope to undo me / Sturdee / you cannot hope /

(He goes out. A silence fills the room. No one moves. At last LUX speaks.)

LUX: All that /
(Pause.)
All that / did you mind it? /
(STURDEE is silent.)
All that / Sturdee / did you? /
(He is unable to reply.)
I ASKED YOU /

STURDEE: Shh /
(LUX bites her lip.)
They're silent / silent the girls /
(He frowns, puzzled. A hiatus, as between life and death, settles over them. At last STURDEE replies to LUX.)
I don't know / Miranda / I don't know /

LUX: You don't know / if you minded it? /

STURDEE: *(At his most introspective.)* I am / as you might be / as Olim is / all three of us / at the very end of things and /
(He tries, and fails to turn to LUX.)
I WISH I COULD SEE /
(He is still, and nurses his neck. The women are silent.)
Arguably / it's better / better I can't /
(He scoffs.)
Elucidation / as the old priests knew / thrives in conditions of obscurity /
(He is urgent.)
I DON'T KNOW / MIRANDA / I DON'T KNOW WHAT SATISFACTION IT GAVE ME /
(Pause.)
I will try to know / I will try / because I will be dead / dead imminently / and it behoves me / to strip out the secret from the heart / or bowels / or whichever part of me / it has so long inhabited / and fling it down / smack / on the

pavement / or the floor / like some snake / ugly
/ or not ugly / the more you look at serpents /
the more they /
(He stops.)
Olim finds me contemptible /

OLIM: I never knew a man so scrupulous / so fastidious
/ in unravelling the mystery of himself / and
so / barren of curiosity regarding anybody
else / including those he claims to love / and
who / while he meditates and speculates / and
hypothesises / are raped / I can't go on / and
raped / and / raped again / I can't go on / I am
not angry / Sturdee / I am not angry / we are
dead / dead and /

STURDEE: Forgive me / Olim /

OLIM: Forgive you? / you can't help yourself /

STURDEE: Forgive me / then /

OLIM: You don't want to be forgiven / Sturdee / you
want us to rejoice in being the stuff of your
conspiracy /

STURDEE: Conspiracy? /

OLIM: Yes / yes / it is a conspiracy /

STURDEE: Against what? / against what am I conspiring? /
(OLIM shakes her head with a profound weariness.)
Yes /
(LUX peels with laughter.)
Yes / I admit it / I have conspired against the
banality of love / the /
(LUX mocks him again.)
Yes / yes / against the mundane and pitiful /

LUX: Thirteen I was /

STURDEE: And circumscribed / and /

LUX: THIRTEEN / STURDEE /

STURDEE: YES / YES / THIRTEEN / SHE WAS /
*(The window in the wall flies open with a crash. The
impact silences them. The head of FLANGE appears in
the aperture, his face awful but resolute.)*

FLANGE: Got one fucker / one /

(OLIM and LUX stare at FLANGE, aghast. STURDEE, unable to turn his head, knows FLANGE by his voice.)

STURDEE: One? /

FLANGE: One / one /
(He shakes his head with horror.)

STURDEE: *(Darkly.)* Which one? /
(FLANGE drops his weapon through the window and scrambles after it.)
WHICH ONE? / FLANGE? /

FLANGE: *(Picking himself up.)* The first of many /
(He strikes the floor with his fists.)
IT CAN BE DONE / IT CAN BE DONE /
(He retrieves his weapon.)
He tied them to a tree / the girls / with plastic cable / red and yellow / a plug on either end / not very expert / and they screamed /

OLIM: We heard them /

FLANGE: How they screamed / a brass band could have marched by playing / he never would have heard it / let alone me /
(He thumps the floor again.)
IT CAN BE DONE / IT CAN BE /
(His jaw is mobile in his triumph.)

STURDEE: Run / Flange /

FLANGE: Run? /

STURDEE: You have a chance / Olim and I / it's over / practically / practically over / we thank you for your loyalty / but killing one /

FLANGE: Not loyalty /

STURDEE: I have to say / can only make the others worse / like wasps / like bees / they swarm / they /

FLANGE: NOT LOYALTY /
(STURDEE is silenced.)

OLIM: *(Replete with sarcasm.)* Mr Sturdee prefers it if we suffer / rather than inflict / atrocity /

FLANGE: *(With a cruel look at her.)* What I do / miss / you may not call / atrocity /
(OLIM looks down.)

	How many are there here? /
STURDEE:	Hundreds /
FLANGE:	HERE? / HUNDREDS HERE? /
	(LUX shrieks with laughter.)
STURDEE:	Not hundreds / not hundreds actually here /
LUX:	I'll tell you how I know /
STURDEE:	Listen / Flange /
LUX:	That I was wearing socks / because I was / short socks /
STURDEE:	Don't interfere /
	(OLIM emits a contemptuous laugh.)
	We are coping / we are / more than coping / we are / to some extent /
OLIM:	*(Mocking.)* WE? / WE? / WE? / ARE COPING? /
STURDEE:	To some extent / achieving a / a / distinct / moral and /
LUX:	White / cotton / ankle socks /
OLIM:	WE / ARE / COPING? / WE? /
STURDEE:	*(To FLANGE.)* JUST FIGHT YOUR SQUALID LITTLE WAR WITH SOMEONE ELSE /
	(He bites his lip.)
	Somewhere else / somewhere / else /
	(A shame descends on FLANGE. His hands hang at his sides.)
OLIM:	Pick up my stick / would you? /
	(FLANGE slowly shakes his head.)
	Flange / if you would be so kind as /
	(He shakes it again, and at last lifts his eyes to OLIM.)
FLANGE:	I can't do that / I think to do that for you /
	(He is at the limit of his thought.)
	I don't know / but I can't do that for you /
OLIM:	I'll fall /
FLANGE:	Yes / probably you will / Miss Olim /
	(He looks at her, now without shame.)
LUX:	All this long bare legs stuff / it isn't true / Sturdee /
FLANGE:	*(Turning violently on LUX.)* SHUT UP / SHUT UP / YOU MAKE ME /

(His fist grips the handle of his weapon.)
LONELY / LONELY /
(His eyes close in his ordeal.)
Lonely /
(LUX is tight-lipped.)
But lonely's all right /
(He goes to STURDEE and stands behind his chair.)
You'll hear me moving / in the rafters / in
the drains / moving and killing / killing for
something which is nothing / nothing at all / to
do with you /
*(He goes to the door and finds it locked. He smiles
thinly and goes to the window by which he entered. He
peers cautiously, then climbs nimbly through.)*

STURDEE:	I rot / I rot / but that's the long run / and in the long run you'll rot / too /
OLIM:	He's gone /
STURDEE:	And to rot / oh / it's an extraordinary condition / believe me /
OLIM:	He's gone / I said /
STURDEE:	Intoxicating / vivid / a passionate chemistry /
LUX:	*(To OLIM.)* I could collect your stick /
OLIM:	You could do / yes /
LUX:	In theory /
OLIM:	In theory? /
	(She shakes her head.)
	Please / pick it up or don't / but spare me your /
STURDEE:	Where's Demonstrator? /
OLIM:	Deliberations / really / is it so much to ask? /
LUX:	Yes /
OLIM:	It is? /
LUX:	Yes /
OLIM:	Then don't do it /
STURDEE:	Look for Demonstrator / somebody /
LUX:	For me / to comfort you / by some little act of common charity /
OLIM:	DON'T DO IT / I SAID /

STURDEE: *(Waspishly.)* THE PAST / THE PAST / SHUT UP ABOUT THE PAST / IT'S NOTHING NOW / LESS THAN NOTHING NOW / LOOK FOR DEMONSTRATOR / PLEASE /
(He trembles.)
Suppose he blundered into Flange? / Flange going / Demonstrator coming in / a horrible collision / was he armed / Flange? / did he have a gun? / an axe? / I couldn't see /
(OLIM laughs at STURDEE's anxiety.)
IT'S FUNNY / IS IT / THAT A MAN LIKE DEMONSTRATOR COULD BE / ELIMINATED / EXPUNGED FROM THE SURFACE OF THE EARTH / BY SOME / SELF-AGGRANDIZING / HEROICIST / LIKE / LIKE /
(LUX, too weak to stand, crawls over the floor on hands and knees towards OLIM's stick.)
It's poverty / it's poverty / Olim / to deride me /
(The door handle is pushed down from the outside, once, twice. OLIM stares at it. LUX looks over her shoulder, frozen. STURDEE senses its significance. On the third occasion, the door simply opens. DEMONSTRATOR enters.)
Thank God /
(DEMONSTRATOR walks in, without haste.)
Thank God /
(He seems distracted.)

DEMONSTRATOR: Song's dead /

STURDEE: I'm sorry /
(He flinches at his own words.)
I think I'm sorry / I'm sorry not for him / but you / it's you I'm sorry for /

DEMONSTRATOR: Of course Song is replaceable /

STURDEE: Yes /

DEMONSTRATOR: Already I have been approached /

STURDEE: Approached? /

DEMONSTRATOR: By others / many envied Song his post / or if not his post / the familiarity with me that the post lent him /

STURDEE: Yes /

DEMONSTRATOR: Some of these may be / let us admit it / better qualified than Song / on the other hand / sheer facility is never enough / skill is one thing / but there is also appetite / some days I think Song was bored /

STURDEE: Or tired / perhaps? /

DEMONSTRATOR: Or tired /

STURDEE: Certainly he was pushed to the limits /

DEMONSTRATOR: Was he? / now it's you who invokes the word /

STURDEE: *(Amused.)* Yes /

DEMONSTRATOR: The word / and the concept / the enormous concept / the little word /

STURDEE: Limitation /

DEMONSTRATOR: Limitation / yes /

STURDEE: First you said it / then I did / it's as if / no matter what our culture / the disparity in our origins / we share this / moral / or intellectual / sense of /
(DEMONSTRATOR has observed LUX reach for OLIM's cane. He goes to her, strips her of it and snaps it across his knee. He tosses the two halves over the floor.)
The frontier /
(OLIM lets out a cry of despair. LUX simply sinks onto her back.)
The frontier is / however/ fixed only so long as imagination condescends to respect it /
(He turns crossly on OLIM.)
DO STOP CRYING / MR DEMONSTRATOR AND I / WE HATE IT /
(STURDEE is swept along by some desperate desire.)
I think we must get on / with or without Mr Song / who was / I think we reluctantly agreed / frequently incompetent / using / for example

	/ coloured cable to tie girls to trees / a plug
	on either end / apparently / scarcely the most
	inspired /
OLIM:	Sturdee /
STURDEE:	Improvisation / given the /
OLIM:	Sturdee /
STURDEE:	HOW LONG HAVE WE GOT / I ASK YOU /

OLIM: Sturdee /

STURDEE: Improvisation / given the /

OLIM: Sturdee /

STURDEE: HOW LONG HAVE WE GOT / I ASK YOU /
(He is grave.)
There is a madman out there / in the garden /
in the fields / guns / swords and things / vicious
and resourceful / I know / he worked for me /
an utter / utter / bigot / what he did to Mr Song
/ I / horribly / horribly /
*(He stops. He looks at DEMONSTRATOR. He sniffs.
He bites his lip. DEMONSTRATOR goes to OLIM. She
lifts her eyes to him, apprehensive, yet not without
hope. STURDEE, sensing the encounter, gazes at the
ceiling. In the excruciating hiatus, LUX cries out.)*

LUX: Hurt Sturdee / hurt Sturdee /

STURDEE: Miranda / Mr Demonstrator is here to punish
all of us / you need not fear he will / somehow /
overlook me / but the curious fact is / if I might
be permitted to revive my musical analogy /
whilst he is evidently strong on composition /
we do not know which instruments he plays / if
any /
(He makes a slight movement of his head.)
Do we? / Mr Demonstrator / know the extent of
your virtuosity? /

DEMONSTRATOR: The cane offended me /

OLIM: Yes /

DEMONSTRATOR: So I broke the cane in two /

OLIM: Yes /

DEMONSTRATOR: The act of breaking the cane was
impetuous /

OLIM: Yes /

DEMONSTRATOR: It seemed infantile / perhaps / to you /

OLIM: *(Resolutely uncritical.)* Oh / I don't know /

DEMONSTRATOR: On the contrary / my revulsion for the cane originated not in some puerile wish to punish you / I think I am correct to insist on this distinction / but to expose you to the essential and inescapable facts of your condition /

OLIM: *(Weakly.)* Yes /

DEMONSTRATOR: A further example of this simultaneously intellectual and visceral reaction to your decay might relate to false teeth / if you have false teeth / oddly I did not discern this earlier / but if you wear them /

(OLIM shakes her head vehemently.)

Throw them away /

(She shakes her head again.)

God's will cannot be thwarted / delayed / perhaps / but in delaying His will by recourse to these devices you render yourself repulsive / do you understand what I am saying? / there was pity in your feebleness / the same applies to this unmarried bride/ the spectacle of her decapitated husband / her murdered entourage / it's /

(He wanders in his ecstasy.)

It's /

(He selects his phrase.)

Entirely necessary /

(He looks at OLIM, who hangs her head.)

At least / so long as we intend to persist with the vain proposition we are human /

(He rests his forehead on OLIM's fragile shoulder.)

Take this once-beautiful woman to the garden / please / and lie there / side by side /

(LUX struggles to her feet, encumbered in her wrecked gown.)

OLIM: Sturdee /

STURDEE: Yes /

OLIM: Our lovely life /

STURDEE: Yes /

OLIM: Our lovely / lovely / life /
STURDEE: Yes /
OLIM: It was / Sturdee /
STURDEE: I'M SAYING / AREN'T I? / I'M SAYING YES /
              (LUX helps OLIM from the room. From the outside her
              cry is a desperate affirmation.)
OLIM: OUR LOVELY LIFE /
              (STURDEE grips the arms of his chair, his gaze
              resolutely fixed to the floor. DEMONSTRATOR looks at
              STURDEE, frowning.)
DEMONSTRATOR: Even now / you sow the seeds of your
              regrets /
STURDEE: Yes /
              (He lifts his gaze.)
              Yes / the woman's as good as dead / as good as
              dead and I /
              (He frowns.)
              What would it have cost me to say a better yes?
              / a better yes than that yes? / nothing /
              (He bites his lip.)
              Only /
DEMONSTRATOR: It flayed her / Sturdee /
STURDEE: Only /
DEMONSTRATOR: It flayed her /
STURDEE: IT FLAYED HER / DID IT / ALL RIGHT /
              SHE WAS FLAYED /
DEMONSTRATOR: It flayed her / still / you preferred her
              suffering to even the mildest compromise with
              your own integrity / at this stage to indulge even
              the smallest lie must hurt / and you hate her /
              I think / therefore / your yes / however poor /
              was probably the nearest thing to affirmation she
              had a right to expect /
STURDEE: It was a madness / a madness of thirty years'
              duration /
DEMONSTRATOR: Yes / and no one / surely / is obliged to
              express gratitude for madness? /
              (STURDEE looks at DEMONSTRATOR.)

FLANGE: Two now /
STURDEE: Two? /
FLANGE: Fuckers / the way they walk / as if you had no
            face /
            *(He kicks the door shut with his foot. It slams
            violently.)*
            I have face /
            (He looks terribly at DEMONSTRATOR.)
            Goodbye to Three /
STURDEE: What makes this so / so very / very /
FLANGE: Down / Three /
            *(He indicates with his head that DEMONSTRATOR
            should kneel on the floor.)*
STURDEE: Sordid and unedifying /
            (FLANGE thrusts DEMONSTRATOR to the floor.)
            Is your determination to turn this miraculous
            encounter / this /
FLANGE: *(Incredulous.)* Miraculous encounter? /
STURDEE: Profoundly spiritual /
FLANGE: Spiritual? /
STURDEE: Transaction / into some filthy episode in a civil
            war /
FLANGE: *(Impatient.)* I must do three / or there won't be
            four /
            (He goes to hack DEMONSTRATOR with his weapon.)
STURDEE: I CAN'T SEE / I CAN'T SEE WHAT YOU'RE
            / WHAT HE'S / FLANGE / PLEASE /
            PLEASE FLANGE / FLANGE / I OWN THIS
            PLACE / YOU SLAVE /
            *(STURDEE senses he has sabotaged his own strategy.
            He is silent. He holds his head stiffly. FLANGE is
            bemused but intransigent. With a studied patience he
            goes to STURDEE and swivels his chair.)*
FLANGE: You corrupt me / you make me /
            (He has no word for his thought.)
            You spoil my spontaneity /
            (STURDEE's gaze rests on FLANGE.)
STURDEE: It's overrated / spontaneity /

(There is a desperate thumping on the locked door. FLANGE is thrown off balance for a moment. He seems to quarrel with himself.)

FLANGE: I kill ugly / your ways / not my ways / I kill ugly /
(FLANGE hacks at the silent DEMONSTRATOR as the door flies open. DOUGHTY and COADE, bound together by the red and yellow cable in a parody of siamese twinship, lurch into the room shrieking and flinging. STURDEE, by the sheer power of his horror, lifts himself on his hands. Outside, a rain of unaimed shots, resounding, ricocheting. STURDEE seems to hang in the air as FLANGE butchers his unresisting victim. The exertion of the act causes him to stagger and to trip. He stays as he falls. DOUGHTY and COADE continue to pitch about the room, but are silent now. They lose energy like a clockwork toy, the sound of their feet less and less percussive. They sink. In the perfect silence which follows, STURDEE slowly descends into his chair.)

STURDEE: You know where the bathroom is /
(FLANGE appears lifeless.)
If you require the bathroom /
(FLANGE is silent.)
And you do / I think / require the bathroom / Flange /
(FLANGE heaves himself up and goes unsteadily in the direction proposed. Seeing the girls motionless in the cable, he stops.)

FLANGE: *(Puzzled.)* I untied these /
(He looks to STURDEE, an expression of profound anxiety on his face.)
I untied these /
(He frowns. STURDEE lifts an open hand in reply. FLANGE goes out. STURDEE's hand falls. He is incapable of movement or thought.)

*

OTHER HOWARD BARKER TITLES

Lot and His God
ISBN: 9781849434096

Scenes from an Execution
ISBN: 9781849434683

The Ecstatic Bible
ISBN: 9781849434171

BLOK/EKO
ISBN: 9781849431101

The Seduction of Almighty God
ISBN: 9781840027112

Slowly / Hurts Given and Received
ISBN: 9781849430166

Dead Hands
ISBN: 9781840024647

The Fence in its Thousandth Year
ISBN: 9781840025712

Barker: Plays One
ISBN: 9781840026122

Barker: Plays Two
ISBN: 9781840026481

Barker: Plays Three
ISBN: 9781840026764

Barker: Plays Four

ISBN: 9781840028515

Barker: Plays Five

ISBN: 9781840028867

Barker: Plays Six

ISBN: 9781840029611

—

A Style and its Origins

by Howard Barker, Eduardo Houth
ISBN: 9781840027181

**Theatre of Catastrophe:
New Essays on Howard Barker**

edited by David Ian Rabey and Karoline Gritzner
HB ISBN: 9781840026948
PB ISBN: 9781840026726

WWW.OBERONBOOKS.COM

Follow us on www.twitter.com/@oberonbooks
& www.facebook.com/oberonbook